THE
POCKET
IDIOT'S
GUIDE TO

Repairing
Your Credit

Second Edition

by Edie Milligan Driskill, CFP, CLU

ALPHA

A member of Penguin Group (USA) Inc.

ALPHA BOOKS

Published by the Penguin Group

Penguin Group (USA) Inc., 375 Hudson Street, New York, New York 10014, USA

Penguin Group (Canada), 90 Eglinton Avenue East, Suite 700, Toronto, Ontario M4P 2Y3, Canada (a division of Pearson Penguin Canada Inc.)

Penguin Books Ltd., 80 Strand, London WC2R 0RL, England

Penguin Ireland, 25 St. Stephen's Green, Dublin 2, Ireland (a division of Penguin Books Ltd.)

Penguin Group (Australia), 250 Camberwell Road, Camberwell, Victoria 3124, Australia (a division of Pearson Australia Group Pty. Ltd.)

Penguin Books India Pvt. Ltd., 11 Community Centre, Panchsheel Park, New Delhi—110 017, India

Penguin Group (NZ), 67 Apollo Drive, Rosedale, North Shore, Auckland 1311, New Zealand (a division of Pearson New Zealand Ltd.)

Penguin Books (South Africa) (Pty.) Ltd., 24 Sturdee Avenue, Rosebank, Johannesburg 2196, South Africa

Penguin Books Ltd., Registered Offices: 80 Strand, London WC2R 0RL, England

Copyright © 2009 by Penguin Group (USA), Inc

International Standard Book Number: 978-159257-950-1
Library of Congress Catalog Card Number: 2009924932

11 10 09   8 7 6 5 4 3 2 1

Interpretation of the printing code: The rightmost number of the first series of numbers is the year of the book's printing; the rightmost number of the second series of numbers is the number of the book's printing. For example, a printing code of 09-1 shows that the first printing occurred in 2009.

Printed in the United States of America

Most Alpha books are available at special quantity discounts for bulk purchases for sales promotions, premiums, fund-raising, or educational use. Special books, or book excerpts, can also be created to fit specific needs.

For details, write: Special Markets, Alpha Books, 375 Hudson Street, New York, NY 10014.

To Allen Driskill, the most creditworthy man I know.

Contents

Appendixes

Introduction

Way back in kindergarten, you learned the importance of playing fair—following the rules—on the playground. For everyone to get along, you knew you needed to play by the rules and that everyone else did, too. If you decided you didn't have to play by the rules, a teacher usually noticed and made you stand in a corner or sent you to the principal's office. If one of your classmates didn't play by the rules, you immediately cried foul. If you were wrongly accused of not playing by the rules, you argued endlessly to protect your good reputation.

Now, as an adult, you have to learn to play on a new playground: the merry-go-round of credit. At first, it seems much more complicated than the playground in kindergarten, but it really isn't. The rules are clearly stated in credit applications, contracts, and laws. People break those rules and cause you harm. And sometimes people report that you misbehaved when you didn't.

Another problem is that this merry-go-round spins with the economy. In the recent downturn, you may have found yourself with a mortgage payment you can't keep current, a car you can't afford, or credit cards that are accumulating late fees. During good times, you followed all the rules and never would have imagined yourself needing to repair a previously perfect credit history.

You probably picked up this book because you know or believe your credit has been damaged.

Only three things could have caused this:

- You didn't understand or didn't follow a rule, and someone noticed.
- Someone else broke a rule using your name.
- Someone reported that you broke a rule when you didn't.

If the first has happened, this book will help you learn the rules and find ways to follow them. Just like back on the playground, sometimes things happen outside of your control, causing you to break a rule. I will help you identify ways to recover from this. I'll also show you how you can design your financial affairs to minimize your chances of having to break a rule in the future.

If the second problem occurred, you are a victim of identity theft, and the thief's actions damaged your credit. If someone pretending to be you transfers all the money out of your bank account, this is called fraud and does not, by itself, damage your credit. However, if because of this, you can't pay your debt payments this month, your credit might be damaged. The growing problem of identity theft is being dealt with by government, corporations, and nonprofit organizations. You will find out what identity thieves look for, learn reasonable steps toward prevention, and discover ways to recover from this difficult form of victimization.

The third problem is the easiest to solve but sometimes the most annoying. You have played by all the rules but somehow are still sent to the principal's office. A bad mark on your credit that is a mistake can be no less damaging than one that reflects totally inappropriate behavior on your part. But the law protects you and helps you get those errors corrected. I'll go through the steps that should help, as well as the actions to take when they don't.

All three of these problems are problems only because an industry has evolved to collect information on our financial affairs. We love it when we want to buy a home and in hours, if not minutes, a mortgage company can preapprove our application, based on information already collected, filed, and ready for review. We hate it when it affects our ability to get a loan, negatively influences the interest rate we must pay for that loan, or causes our application for a credit card to be rejected.

The challenge comes when we don't want our credit history so readily available. For instance, complaints have surfaced recently over a practice in which your credit card company can periodically pull your credit report and then raise your interest rate or cancel your account based on the history of other accounts you maintain. Back to the playground, this would be like misbehaving on the swings and then not being allowed to play on the slide either. A teacher might be very justified in expecting that your behavior would be the same on both pieces of equipment. But is it reasonable for your credit card company to draw the same conclusion?

Over the years since the credit-reporting industry has been in business, consumers have often cried foul at many of the behaviors of the industry. Consumers, a.k.a. voters, have run to their legislators who, in turn, have passed laws to keep the industry from running amuck. Too many consumers have been judged as not creditworthy due to errors on their reports. The creditors don't really like this, either, because they profit from being able to identify good potential customers. If tomorrow all consumers had a bad credit report, they'd have a hard time knowing whom to do business with.

A set of laws has been enacted at the federal level, and I explore them in Chapter 12. It is helpful to understand what the credit-reporting industry and its customers, the creditors, are really allowed to do. Chances are, if you feel they are acting unfairly, others feel the same way. Every day lawsuits are filed in an attempt to enforce these laws, and every day big-name corporations are fined or sanctioned. Reporting systems are in place to collect these experiences and help keep these companies from overstepping their bounds.

With the credit-reporting industry seeming to be a freight train running down the track with no brakes, an alter industry sprang up to fight back. Collectively known as the credit-repair industry, companies that promise to clean up your credit report for a fee have been around for more than 25 years. They immediately attracted attention as scams, so legislators created another body of laws designed to keep them under control. Aside from the money they took from consumers who believed their claims, they did a deeper disservice. For a time, some people believed that the solution to debt problems was to file bankruptcy and then hire one of these firms to take that reference off their credit report.

This type of firm might use one of several strategies to return you to a clean report. I cover the different strategies and ways to spot scams in Chapter 10. There certainly are legitimate counseling and advisory firms that charge fees to help you review your report and develop a strategy for improving your credit, and you'll find information about these organizations and individuals in Chapter 11. They may also provide dispute services and other helpful advice. As you evaluate the strategies covered in this book, you might find it beneficial to hire someone to help you reduce the amount of time you'll spend repairing your credit. But you should be able to do it yourself with the advice in the following chapters.

It is possible to function in our world without good credit, and millions of Americans are coping with this reality every day. However, it is expensive and inconvenient. Building a good credit history, protecting it, and using it to enhance your financial standing are all skills you'll have after reading this book. Some credit problems have quick fixes, but credit planning is a thoughtful process that will pay off repeatedly as you enjoy the power that comes with a reputation of creditworthiness.

How to Use This Book

This book is intended to both give you a general understanding of the credit-reporting industry and help you develop a specific game plan for managing your own credit report. It's important to gain that general understanding, explained in the early chapters, before you set out to take any specific steps, which I detail in later chapters. I also encourage you to read through the sections about issues you might not have experienced, such as identity theft, to help you learn to prevent possible future problems with your report.

Extras

Throughout the book you'll encounter the following extras, which expand on key points and offer additional advice, alert you to cautions, or define terms used in the credit industry.

To Your Credit

These sidebars give you quick tips on enhancing your creditworthiness and making your way through the complicated world of credit reporting.

Credit Cautions

Be aware of these warnings as you build your report or repair one already damaged.

def•i•ni•tion

Look for these definitions to explain terms the industry uses that might not be familiar to you.

Acknowledgments

This book is an outgrowth of more than 20 years of working as a financial counselor with consumers facing credit challenges. Their frustration with their own choices and resolve to find more effective ways to handle credit taught me what worked and what didn't. I would like to thank them for their trust in me to help them through those difficult times so that I could share their insights with you.

I'd like to thank the many representatives of the credit grantors, credit reporters, credit counselors, and credit repairers around the country who helped me develop accurate and timely information for this book. Specifically, thanks to Rob Griffin at Experian, Darrell Knabb at Innovis, Jason Nierman at TransUnion, David Rubinger at Equifax, and Consuelo Jones at the Chapter 13 Trustee for the southern district of Ohio.

Special thanks to my family and friends who now recognize these long absences while I disappear to write.

Trademarks

All terms mentioned in this book that are known to be or are suspected of being trademarks or service marks have been appropriately capitalized. Alpha Books and Penguin Group (USA) Inc. cannot attest to the accuracy of this information. Use of a term in this book should not be regarded as affecting the validity of any trademark or service mark.

Potential Credit Pitfalls

In This Chapter

- Identifying situations that lead to most credit problems
- How your credit report reveals these problems
- How divorce impacts credit reports

Your consumer reports are collections of information gathered primarily by three leading companies: Experian, Equifax, and TransUnion. Then a company called Fair Isaacs analyzes and translates this information into a number called a credit score. These reports will undoubtedly hold information that is both fact and fiction. Either can look good or bad to the customers of these reports: potential creditors, employers, or insurers. If bad information is untrue, it won't stay around long. If bad information is true, your situation caused it. So let's take a look at the major reasons people end up with reports which look bad to the businesses that buy credit reports.

Watch Out for Dings: Negative Credit Indicators

Understanding what types of financial decisions will result in credit problems is the first step toward building a good *credit history*. *Dings* on your report will remain as long as they are legally allowed (usually seven years) before they're removed, but understanding how they got there in the first place is the key.

def•i•ni•tion

A **credit history** is a summary of the manner in which a consumer has handled credit contracts. It reflects how much he borrows, whether he makes payments on time, and how much he still owes. A **ding** is an indicator on a credit report that some or all companies looking at the report might find negative. It could be a late payment or even the number of times your report was purchased by creditors (too many inquiries looks bad).

Many circumstances can seem totally out of your control. A divorce, a layoff, or a sudden illness can leave a once-perfect credit report riddled with dings within a matter of months. Even though you can't always control these events, you can take steps to control their impact on your credit. How you manage your debt and savings will determine, to a great extent, how well you survive an unexpected bump on your financial road.

Money-Management Mistakes

In my 20 years as a financial counselor, I have met with thousands of individuals feeling tremendous financial stress. But I've never met a person who woke up one morning and declared, "I'm going to screw up my credit today!" Everyone, without exception, makes the best decisions he can make on each day he sets out to tackle all the complexities of life.

Many factors feed into financial decisions; the funny thing is, very few of these factors are about money. They could stem from social pressure to keep a wardrobe stocked with new and expensive clothes, to buy a new car every other year, or to buy more house than we can afford. Or they can stem from emotional or psychological problems, such as depression, causing a mental perspective that doesn't allow someone to consider how actions taken today might have an impact for years down the road.

Of course, we sometimes make decisions that we would never have made if we had been better informed of the consequences. But even these decisions can involve personal or social factors. For instance, a decision to move to a neighborhood to access better schools for your children could be influenced by a builder's offer that makes a home seem more affordable than it is. By helping you qualify for a mortgage where the payments would eventually rise to an unaffordable level, the builder satisfied your social need to be in a school district acceptable to you.

Managing your personal finances is a complicated process. You can't change most of the decisions you've made up to this point. However, you can look back at those decisions knowing what you know now and try to determine whether you would've made different choices. Taking that awareness forward will make you a more effective decision maker in the future. So let's consider some of the choices that can lead to credit or collection problems.

Overspending

Nobody ever walked into my office and announced, "I spend too much money." Instead, I've usually heard, "I don't buy anything *extra*." I believed these clients because if they thought it was extra, they wouldn't be interested in buying it. What they needed to do was rein in their definition of the word *extra*. Financial planners like to talk about the differences between wants and needs, but that implies there is a clear line which someone other than the consumer can draw. Each person has a set of personal preferences: what we buy is a need; what we don't buy is a want.

Think about your own definition of *extra*. What did you buy that pushed up your credit card balances and that others might not have purchased? Do you ever find yourself looking at cash balances in your checking account and wanting to spend it all before next payday? Remember, these decisions aren't always about money. We sometimes use money to feel better, impress others, or live up to some expectations that we have about success.

To Your Credit

Sometimes the richest neighbors are those who appear to be the most conservative with money. Trying to keep up with those who have the nicest homes and the newest cars can lead to more debt and less financial security in the long run.

How can spending be overspending if we have the cash in hand to do it? Most of the time, we are very aware of our immediate needs: today's lunch, gas to get to work, or a movie rental tonight. What we forget are the midterm needs: next month's school fees, our kids' next pairs of shoes, or the next car repair. Credit problems can start when we let our short-term spending take priority over these midterm needs. When those midterm needs come due, as they always do, we find ourselves short of cash and end up having to pay a bill late or use a credit card to fund them.

Overdebting

Marketing specialists know we will spend between 5 and 15 percent more on an average shopping trip if we use a credit card instead of cash. Try it sometime. Go to the store with a shopping list and the cash you intend to spend instead of your credit card. Watch yourself put back things you are tempted to buy or even cross things off your list that are not really necessary.

Overdebting happens when a person fails to make the connection between the purchase made with the credit and the money it will take to repay the debt. You might have heard yourself rationalize, "It won't add but a few dollars to the monthly payment." The reality is that a $100 purchase on a credit card can cost you up to $700 in payments over the years. Would you have bought that item if it had a $700 price tag on it? Did your brain actually put a $2 price tag on it because that is the amount your payment would increase each month?

At some point, buying on credit can lead to a budget that has almost all available cash going out to minimum payments on credit cards, leaving necessities to be financed on these same cards. This means running up the balances even more. With most *creditors*, when you reach a level of debt that equals about half of your annual income, the creditor will deny you any more open credit. So if you have an income of $60,000, you might find yourself in $30,000 of debt before you are denied new credit.

def•i•ni•tion

> The **creditor** or credit grantor is an individual or a business that extends a consumer/debtor a loan or line of credit. Sometimes this company is not the company servicing or collecting the payments on the debt.

You might still have so-called perfect credit. You make all your payments on time, and all your accounts are open and in good standing. You just can't get any new accounts. This situation can eventually lead to bad credit because the first time you have a sudden need, such as a car repair, you'll spend money you intended to send to a credit card company as a payment. That payment, in turn, will become late and might affect your credit reference for that account. And so the cycle of bad credit begins.

Some financial strategists say the solution to this problem is to refinance. This really means spreading the existing debt over a longer period of time, sometimes pledging collateral to do it. Although refinancing can help relieve the current cash-flow pressure, it usually does not change your behavior by itself. Your need to begin saving for the midterm needs is still there; if you don't begin aggressively finding ways to fund these needs, you'll end up using debt the next time those midterm needs come due.

New debt is rarely the solution to old debt. But just like an alcoholic's outlook, it seems that a drink will be the solution to the hangover. At the time, it is; it just compounds the problem in the long run.

Too Much House

The American dream is not to own a home. The American dream is to qualify for a home you never thought you could afford. But if you thought you couldn't afford it, you probably can't. Real estate agents and mortgage brokers are salespeople, not financial planners. They are paid commissions on how much they can sell you. If you default on the mortgage loan five years later, it doesn't affect their paycheck. It's your problem, not theirs.

In *The Pocket Idiot's Guide to Mortgages* (Alpha Books, 2003), I walk you through a process to determine how much home you can afford. It's essential that you do this before you ask mortgage lenders how much money they will lend you. When a lender says "You can have up to $250,000," what he should be saying is "We would be happy to have you pay us $500,000 over the next 30 years."

I remember my parents buying a home in 1970 that happened to have an old pool in the backyard. I was excited until I learned that (1) *I was going to be in charge of cleaning the pool*, and (2) *we weren't going to take vacations anymore because the pool would cost about the same amount of money to maintain*. It's hard to make financial sacrifices—such as giving up vacations—to get something you want. Your instinct is to want to continue spending money on what you have always spent money. It's even worse if you're moving up to a richer neighborhood because you'll feel pressure to upgrade other aspects of your lifestyle, which means spending even more money.

In addition, we often forget about the upkeep and repairs involved in owning a house. We all want to believe that we've found the perfect house and nothing will ever go wrong, but the reality is furnaces go bad, roofs need to be replaced, and chimneys need to be swept—and these all cost money. If you don't have the cash to pay for repairs and maintenance outright, you'll have to finance them, which means even more debt. And so the cycle continues.

Too Much Car

Many families are drawn into more car than they can afford, succumbing to advertising, self-esteem, and peer pressure. Lenders who allow loans greater than the value of the car, car leasing, and buy-here, pay-here contracts have all contributed in their own way to worsening credit reports for many consumers. Cars can be one of the most expensive items in a family's budget, and having good credit can be critical to acquiring a reliable vehicle.

It's very easy to spend more money on a car and borrow more for it than really fits into your budget. Lenders even allow us to become *upside down* on a loan as well, meaning we owe more on a car than it is worth. They even allow people to roll that difference into a new loan, creating yet another upside-down loan on the next car.

def•i•ni•tion

Being **upside down** on a car loan means you owe more than the car is worth. This puts you in a tremendous bind if the car is wrecked. The insurance carrier will pay only the value of the car, not the payoff on the loan. Insurance that covers this gap—called gap insurance—is available. You should look into gap insurance if you are already in this situation, but, better yet, avoid this situation altogether.

People rarely pay cash for cars these days. Most people finance them. Leasing became popular in the 1990s as a way for automakers to sell more expensive cars to people who couldn't afford them. This form of long-term car-rental contract became popular, and people got used to more luxurious cars. Many times, the mileage restrictions leave people owing more at the end of the lease than they have cash to pay. It's a snowball effect that often ends in bad credit marks.

The entire "buy here, pay here" industry is an outgrowth of the huge numbers of consumers who find themselves unable to finance a car because of bad credit. The embedded finance charges for these cars are usually terribly high. They don't have regular interest contracts; instead, they mark up the sales price of the car to double or triple its value and then let you pay it off over time. The extra interest and expensive repairs often needed for these cars put pressure on the rest of the budget and can contribute to more credit problems.

Lack of Savings

It might sound old-fashioned to say that having a savings account can help you keep your credit good, but it's true. To help you understand why a savings account is so important, let's first look at what happens when you don't have some cash stashed away.

Let's say you plan out your cash flow over your next few paychecks like most working people do. You set aside money to pay your bills, pay down your debts, and pay for food, gas, and entertainment. If you're like most folks, you wouldn't be able to buy a new refrigerator with what is left. But if your fridge dies next week, you'll be out looking for a new one whether you can afford to pay for it or not. Now consider two different scenarios: if you had been regularly setting aside money for home repairs, you'd be able to tap into your savings to pay for a new refrigerator. If you hadn't been saving, however, you'd have to go into debt to buy it, perhaps by signing a 90-day same-as-cash loan agreement. You'd promise yourself you'd pay it off before the interest begins, but that might become harder than you anticipated, and you'd probably end up paying the 25 percent interest and adding another $35 payment to your monthly budget. Had you been saving the $35 in advance, you wouldn't be in more debt.

This is the cycle many Americans find themselves in and that led to their credit problems in the first place. It is very common and very frustrating. In later chapters, I explore solutions to stopping the cycle and getting back in control of your savings and your debt.

Lack of Income

Workers are always changing jobs in our economy. Many times it is within the same employer with no disruption of pay and benefits. If a worker decides it is time for a new job and finds one at a new employer, she will usually try very hard to make sure there is very little disruption to her income flow. Problems can erupt, however, when the worker is terminated and has not had time to plan.

Insurance products such as unemployment benefits, disability insurance, and life insurance make a huge difference in how people get through unplanned periods of no income. Without exception, those with low debt and high personal savings will get through a period of no income with fewer credit problems.

Layoff

The federal unemployment insurance program covers most workers who lose a job due to no fault of their own. This program is funded by employers and gives workers a percentage of their previous income for six months while they locate new employment. In most cases, however, the payment is much less income than a laid-off worker needs to pay basic obligations.

Credit Cautions

A credit card is not an emergency fund. Sure, you can use it in a pinch to buy time until you get to your emergency cash, but don't be fooled. A time of lower income or unexpected expenses is the last time you want to be running up your credit card balances. Save regularly for emergencies and protect your credit.

If the unemployment period drags on and other sources of income or substantial savings are not available, an unemployed person will be unable to pay any bills. When a payment is more than 30 days late, it appears on the person's credit report. If the payment is more than a few months late, *collection* actions begin—maybe even repossessions and lawsuits. All these consequences eventually are reported on your credit report.

Some creditors understand that these temporary problems do not truly reflect underlying creditworthiness and take into consideration such extenuating circumstances when reviewing credit reports. People are even allowed to add a statement to their credit report explaining the situation. I discuss the writing and placement of consumer statements in Chapter 7.

Since the widespread adoption of computerized credit approvals, more and more creditors rely solely on credit scores, like FICO, to measure your creditworthiness and determine the interest rate to offer you. Recent dings will weigh more heavily in this score than those that have aged a bit.

def•i•ni•tion

Collection is a term creditors commonly use to define the activities needed to manage an account that has fallen behind in payments. To be sent to collection or to be in collection might mean that the account has changed departments within the company or has been sent outside the company to be pursued for payment. Once an account has been sent to collection, the debtor might receive different types of statements, letters, and phone calls requesting payment and threatening legal action.

Disability

The good news is that the medical profession has found more ways to keep us alive. The bad news is that, even though we might survive more car wrecks and catastrophic illnesses, our periods of disability when we can't work are increasing. Most workers in the United States are underinsured for this risk. Many employers who cover their workers for disability insurance cover only 60 percent of their wages or only six months of disability. The 40 percent gap in income is devastating to most families, especially during a time of increased medical costs.

Credit problems occur during a period of disability for two reasons. First, the family might turn to open credit accounts to cover unaffordable expenses while disabled. The thinking is that they can pay back those charges when the worker goes back to work. Sometimes that strategy works, but if the budget was tight before the disability, it only leads to greater stress in the long run. Second, the existing credit accounts might fall behind in payments during the period of decreased income.

Business Failure

We live in a country of entrepreneurs, and we value the opportunity to start and grow businesses. To endorse this entrepreneurial spirit, Congress long ago enacted bankruptcy laws to protect people who take risks and fail. These laws allow us to reorganize our payments or be relieved of our obligations to repay certain debts. Without the bankruptcy laws to catch us when we fall, few people would dare to begin a business.

Since a personal signature must back most debt incurred to start a business, this debt can find its way to the entrepreneur's credit report. And if the debt is not repaid in a timely fashion, the dings will show up there as well. When a business fails, the entrepreneur likely will take a huge hit personally, going without income for some time. This will impact other obligations—obligations that are also reported to the credit bureaus.

Divorce

Early in my financial-counseling practice, I noticed a direct relationship between divorce and credit problems. I used to joke that adding another mortgage payment to the budget is not usually the solution to a tight budget, but that is what often happens when couples split into two households. Financial problems is one of the top reasons for divorce in our country. It's also true that divorce is one of the top reasons for bankruptcy.

The turmoil and stress of many divorces divert attention from managing finances well. People going through divorce make decisions under pressure and often without complete information. Many divorce decrees don't fully consider the impact the financial arrangements will have on a credit report.

In addition, couples going through a divorce might not be coordinating payments or other account-management activities as well as they should be. They also might be incurring more expenses to accomplish the divorce, diverting cash away from servicing accumulated debt. I've even seen temporary court orders that strip one party of the ability to make even minimum payments on existing accounts.

It's a difficult time, with many changes coupled with a lot of hasty decisions. It is understandable that some of this turmoil would eventually be reflected on the credit report.

Whose Debt Is Whose?

When making the tough decisions that divorce always forces upon people, it's important to ask whose credit report will reflect the difficulties. The answer is simple: whoever signed for the debt. A divorce decree can grant an asset, such as a financed boat, to the husband. It can also order the husband to pay the remaining payments on the installment loan. But if the wife signed or co-signed the original loan, that payment history will show on her credit report. If the husband stops making payments, the bank will call her and eventually sue her for the balance due after it repossesses the boat. The divorce decree means nothing to the bank. If the ex-wife does cough up some money to make that debt good, she can then sue her ex-husband for repayment, but her credit report has already taken the hit.

Credit Cautions

A divorce decree does not change existing contracts with your creditors. You are liable for any contracts you have signed, regardless of what arrangements are ordered by the divorce court. Keep that in mind as you divide up the bills left from the marriage.

The Least You Need to Know

- Your credit report is a reflection of your financial behavior; you have control over much of that behavior.

- Just because you qualify for a credit account doesn't mean you can afford it.

- Having a strong savings plan for midterm and emergency items is one of the most powerful strategies you can put in place to protect your credit rating.

- Several events—such as a layoff, disability, and divorce—that can impact your credit report negatively are outside of your immediate control, but you can take steps to minimize their impact on your credit.

2

Bad Things That Happen to Good Credit Reports

In This Chapter

- Ways your creditors can mess up your report
- Spotting mistakes credit bureaus make
- Understanding the consequences of identity theft

When it comes to their finances, millions of Americans never do anything wrong. They always pay their bills on time and never get sick, lose a job, or start an unsuccessful business. You've met them, right? Well, even if you *try* to do things right, your credit report can still get dinged! Your financial transactions pass through at least a couple of hundred computers and who knows how many human hands before it gets to your report. Imagine the possibilities for mistakes! And don't forget the chance that someone might actually try to mess up your report on purpose.

We all have to live with our credit reports, but we don't have to live with the mistakes on them. Learning what mistakes can happen and how is the first step to understanding how proactive you need to be in managing your report. In this chapter, you learn how mistakes happen and who's responsible.

Mistakes Made by Creditors

Rule No. 1 in credit transactions is this: you are the customer. With the amount of competition for your business, you should be made to feel like a very valued customer. But when the companies' policies and procedures filter down to the last customer service representative hired or the trillionth bit of data shuffled around that day, they may forget this important point. It then becomes your job to remind them. The most frustrating part about this challenge is that if a company has actually damaged your credit report—even temporarily—you might not be able to take your business elsewhere until the problem is fixed. It's like a tire dealer letting the air out of your tires until you buy new tires from him.

To Your Credit

If you start out life believing your credit report will always have some errors on it, you'll never be disappointed. Looking for them could turn into a game!

How can this happen when computers don't decide on their own to lie? The real truth is that the people in charge of them usually don't make conscious decisions to mess up your credit report, either. But it does happen. The following sections detail a few situations that commonly cause problems.

But Computers Don't Lie!

A credit card you paid off just never gets the final payoff recorded properly and starts to report as late. Your car loan company makes you an offer to pass a payment at Christmastime, but the computer forgets to register that you accepted, so all payments after that are reported as one month late.

Most of the time, these mistakes become obvious to you on a monthly statement or through additional correspondence or phone calls from the creditor. You might or might not be looking closely enough to see them. Or you might dismiss them as the "crossed in the mail" type of problems. The good news is that since creditors usually report a late payment only when it becomes more than 30 days late, you have some time to respond before it affects your *consumer file*.

def•i•ni•tion

> A **consumer file** is a record of all the credit histories a credit-reporting agency collects on a specific person, along with that person's employment, address, and public records histories.

However, it's not a bad idea to keep records of all correspondence and phone calls about any problem. Then check your credit reports a couple months later to make sure the mistake didn't hit the credit reference. I always recommend the efficiency of checking your report yearly. It is so frustrating to try to go back two or three years and prove that payments on an account were all made in a timely manner. Even if you keep all your bills and cancelled checks and have them organized beautifully, it takes time to sort it all out.

Account Number Changes

If you lose your wallet or even suspect someone might have your credit card numbers, call your credit companies and tell them. They won't cancel your account but will simply give it a different account number. They'll send you a new card, which you will activate using their secure system. And all is well again.

Sometimes your account number changes because your credit card company decides to reorganize its internal system. Without any notice, it sends you a new card and tells you to tear up the old ones. There shouldn't be any problem, right?

What happens to your credit report when these numbers change? You will have two credit references where there used to be one: a reference to the old, now closed, account and a reference to the account with the new number. The report should indicate the old account was closed or transferred to a new account for a good reason, and it should

show a zero balance and no late payments during
the transition period. It should also show the date
you opened the first account because old accounts
favorably impact your report, while recently
opened accounts can be a negative influence. If
you see something like "Account Closed By Credit
Grantor," this usually indicates some inappropriate
action on your part and is a ding on your report. It's
important that you get this statement removed if it
was applied incorrectly.

To Your Credit

Keep open only credit accounts you
know you'll be able to track. The more
credit references you have on your
report, the more opportunities for error
there are.

In addition, make sure you are referencing the
appropriate (new) account number when you make
payments. If you have an online or telephone bill-
payment service send your payments, you need
to change your account number with the service.
Payments that go in under the old number will be
difficult to reconcile if your new account reflects
past-due payments.

Loans Bought and Sold

When you borrow money, three parties usually are
involved in the transaction: you, the source of the

money, and the company that collects the payments for them. In many cases, the last two are the same company, but that's not always true. Throughout the life of the loan, whether it is a mortgage, a car loan, or another installment loan, these parties can change. Your loan can be sold to a new lender or passed to a new company for servicing.

Even if the parties never actually change, the bank that issued the loan might change its name. Or perhaps a bank will shift the servicing of its loans from one division to another. If the credit-reporting companies aren't made aware of these changes, they can make a mess of your credit report. Ten years after buying a $100,000 home, it can look like you owe $500,000 on it if the old mortgage companies haven't properly reported the subsequent sales of your loan. And 10 years later, these folks are hard to find.

The credit bureau will clean it up for you, and new creditors know this happens sometimes, so don't panic. However, it will require some effort on your part and might take a couple of months to resolve. This makes it imperative that you begin looking at your report months before you intend to purchase a home if you haven't already been monitoring it regularly.

Credit Cautions

Watch out when your mortgage servicing is sold to a new company. The new company might not record your last on-time payment with the old company, and your credit report might show you as delinquent (meaning not paid per the terms of the loan). Check your report two to three months after the new company assumes the loan, to make sure that the reporting is accurate. If it is not, challenge it right away while you still have easy access to the records.

Mistakes by Credit Bureaus

Imagine someone taking out a billboard to wish you a happy birthday and misspelling your name, or a doctor walking into the emergency room with the chart of the patient next door. What if the furnace repairman came to your home with the wrong part to fix your furnace? The typist at the billboard company, the nurse at the emergency room, and the receptionist at the repair company didn't check their work. They didn't say, "Let me read that back to you."

When credit bureaus get a new piece of information on you, they never call you to say, "Let me read this back to you." However, they'll be happy to sell you a service that notifies you when something is added to your report. Each of their websites has extensive information describing these services, and some consumers find them valuable. Even if you do subscribe to a service, it's still your responsibility to read your report to determine whether what has been added is correct or a mistake. Here are some of the most common mistakes.

Mistaken Identity or Similar Names

Sometime, for fun, do a simple Internet search on your name and just look at how many people have the same name as you, or at least a similar one. If you are lucky enough to have a mother who misspelled your name so badly in the delivery room that no one could ever have the same one, send her a card and thank her. Chances are, you won't be getting other people's *credit references* in your file. But if your creditors have misspelled your name or transposed your Social Security number, all your information might end up in someone else's file—or, worse yet, someone else's information might end up in yours.

def•i•ni•tion

A **credit reference** is an individual or a business that has loaned a consumer money and reports the details of that account to a credit bureau.

Mistaken identity happens most frequently with family members who have only a middle initial to distinguish them from each other. If you've experienced this, the sad news is it will probably keep happening. You'll need to be more diligent than most to keep your report clean of references you don't own. If the other person has good credit behavior, it might not affect you until your outstanding credit appears to get too high, so always check the report a few weeks before you apply for credit. You might also want to attach a standard letter to any credit application warning a potential creditor that it might encounter references that aren't yours.

You might also find that your credit report contains references to bad debts on which you were the *co-signer* for someone else, such as a family member. You might not even be aware your family member has reneged on the obligation until it is too late to protect your credit report. You can prevent this by asking the creditor to send bills and late notices to you as well as to the primary signer. You can also call the creditor if you have the account number and get the payment status through automated response systems.

def•i•ni•tion

The **co-signer** of a loan is the person who is contractually obligated to pay back a debt if the primary signer is unable to make the payments on time.

Credit Cautions

Signing a lease for an adult child to get him started in an apartment might seem like a loving thing to do, but when his roommate skips out, you'll be responsible for that half of the rent, and you'll end up paying or having your credit damaged or both. Co-sign only obligations you are ready to pay.

Just Plain Mistakes

Errors that are just plain mistakes are usually the easiest to fix. Because these errors will be impossible for the credit bureau to verify, by law, the credit bureau will have to remove them from your report (see Chapter 7). The other nice thing about random mistakes is that they are random and probably won't reappear. Once you fix them, you're done. Of course, you could see a whole new batch of them at any time.

A word of warning is in order here: just because you don't recognize a company's name doesn't mean you don't have an account with that company. For instance, you might have opened a credit card at a local department store, and the card has the name of the store on it. The bill, however, says Consolidated Finance, and this is the creditor listed on your credit report. Usually, you can use account numbers to solve these mysteries. Keep a list of your account numbers handy, and remember that sometimes the reports truncate the numbers for security reasons.

Previously Corrected Errors

Few things are more frustrating than spending time correcting a problem you didn't cause in the first place, only to have it pop up again a few months later.

If the same mistake shows up on your credit report, chances are good that the fault lies with the creditor, who continues to submit the information incorrectly, rather than the credit bureau. Either way, it is very frustrating when a problem you think you've fixed comes back. In Chapter 7, I cover strategies for attacking this annoying problem.

Identity Theft

When someone has information about you (such as your address, Social Security number, and bank account number) and uses it to pretend to be you and to harm you in the process, the crime is called identity theft. The usual purpose for this charade is to use your good credit to steal money. The identity thief might open a new credit card in your name, immediately change the address to a post office box so you never see a bill, and then cash-advance thousands of dollars on it and never make the payments. Eventually, your credit report would reflect the late payments on this account. You might learn about this only after a collector tracks you down with a phone call or another credit card raises your interest rate because of a bad reference on your credit report.

To Your Credit _____

The National Fraud Information Center at www.fraud.org is a hotline that refers fraud complaints to the appropriate enforcement agency. It also provides information on how to protect yourself from fraud.

These activities have always been illegal and have been generally referred to as fraud or theft. The term "identity theft" is relatively new, and even newer are the laws that make it specifically illegal. It is rare to find someone who has been convicted of this crime because the person must have a fraud conviction first. Just pretending to be someone is not a crime unless you harm him or her by doing so. But once a prosecutor has secured a fraud conviction, the criminal is going to jail, and the prosecutor needs to move on to his next case.

What a Pain!

Legislators in my state and others are passing new laws against identity theft, in part because being victimized in this way is very unnerving. If you've ever had an intruder in your home (whether or not that person harmed you or took anything), it probably sent you into a difficult emotional state. You might have been jumpy for months, imagined people in the bushes, and had bad dreams. Intruders in your bank account or credit file are no less unsettling, and they can potentially take much more from you. Carrying off your big-screen TV takes some serious effort, but filling out a form or typing a few keystrokes can move thousands of dollars out of your financial accounts.

Get Ready for a Fight

Identity theft is one of those totally un-American situations in which you are considered guilty until you take a lot of action to prove yourself innocent. If you've never had seriously bad credit and this happens to you, you'll find yourself having conversations that you've never imagined having. In Chapter 9, I explain in detail how to guard against identity theft and what to do if you are ever victimized. The big credit bureaus all have processes in place and special hotlines to help you sort it all out.

It will be difficult to show your credit file to anyone until this is all settled, which could take months. In the meantime, you'll have a lot of explaining to do to everyone who must see it—and they might not believe you right away. This is another compelling reason to check your report regularly. Not only will the reports alert you to something potentially damaging going on, but you will also have recent good reports to show the "before and after" views to people with whom you would like to do business.

The Least You Need to Know

- Doing everything right is no guarantee your creditors and the credit bureau will report it correctly.

- Credit references can be very confusing, with accounts being bought and sold like hot potatoes.

- You are the only person who knows enough about your financial dealings to spot credit-reporting errors efficiently.

- The better your credit is, the more likely you will look like a good target for identity thieves.

3

What Is Credit?

In This Chapter

- How creditors use credit scores to determine whom they do business with
- The major components of creditworthiness
- Deciding what kind of credit you need

Recently, I purchased a present on eBay, the online auction house. A few days later, this e-mail arrived:

Have you looked at your eBay I.D. recently? There's a new number beside it. Someone who's done business with you on eBay gave you a positive feedback comment. Way to go!

Why is positive feedback so important on eBay? Feedback is the cornerstone of trading on eBay. Your positive feedback is like a stamp of approval. It tells other community members what it's like to do business with you, which builds trust across all aspects of your trading on eBay. The more you do business in a responsible way on eBay, the greater your feedback number—and your eBay reputation—will be.

Boy, did I feel proud! Not only did I do something right, but others will also know that I did. On eBay, they call it feedback. Your creditors call it an *account rating*. Even though there are very few consequences to damaging your reputation on eBay, the principle is the same as damaging your reputation with your creditors. If you behave well, they tell the world, and future creditors are more likely to trust you. If you behave badly, they also tell the world, and you have a harder time getting future creditors to trust you.

def•i•ni•tion

> **Account rating** is a term used by creditors to refer to the relative status of your account with them. Each creditor might have its own internal rating system.

Credit Scoring

Years ago, if your great-grandfather needed a loan, he walked into his local bank and sat down with a banker who might have known him since he was in knickers. Credit granting was a personal service offered to known customers. As the credit industry grew to be more impersonal, credit reports became a way for a prospective creditor to get to know an individual quickly. As personal finances became more complicated and likewise made one's report more complicated, a new service was born called credit scoring. Scoring is a process that uses a mathematical formula with variables found on a credit report and solves for a number called a credit score. Fair Isaacs is the first company to become successful at this service and continues to be the leader, although they do have some competition.

FICO is an acronym for Fair Isaacs Company, which sells credit scoring services to creditors. Because your credit files may be different at the three major credit-reporting agencies, the resulting scores will be different when the formula is applied to each report. To complicate this further, Fair Isaacs sells different formulas and recently changed their formula to be more predictive of your payment behavior. It is almost impossible for you to know which scoring tool a potential creditor is using.

Trustworthiness

Think about your friends and family members. Some you would trust your life with, and with others, loaning $5 to them means you'll never see that money again. You know who is trustworthy; you've watched them for years. You probably rely on other behaviors to make this distinction. Do they show up when and where they promise to be? Do they offer help to you when you need it? Do they seem to manage their affairs without constant high drama?

Humans seem to be the only species that develops trust in each other. Dogs come in a distant second, but even they don't trust each other. Imagine a dog "lending" another dog a biscuit and expecting to get it back with interest some day. But humans do that every day. We have our pay automatically deposited into a faceless institution, run by humans we've never met. We are technically loaning our money to our bank, expecting to get it back when we want it. Depending upon how long we are willing to live without it, the bank will promise to return it to us with interest.

What causes you to develop trust in a bank, an insurance company, or an investment firm? How do you define trustworthiness? If they fail on a promise to you, do you take your business elsewhere? Do you base your attitudes on their advertising, their interior decorating, or the professionalism of their employees? Or do you merely trust your government to regulate them and protect you? Marketing experts around the world study these factors, looking for the edge to earn your trust and get your business.

The main question to ask yourself when you think about developing a trustworthy image is, *would you do business with you?* Knowing everything you know about how you make decisions, how you fulfill promises, and how you treat other people, would you loan you money? If not, think about the things you need to change to achieve that image.

Credit Markets

Imagine you are the CEO of a huge bank. You have convinced the wage-earning and asset-owning public that you are trustworthy. They like your advertising, your color scheme, your employee attitudes, your product names, and your community service projects. People are depositing hundreds of millions of dollars into your bank every year. Now what do you do?

You need to find people who will borrow this money and pay you interest so that you can pay your employees, your advertising agency, and the interest due to your depositors. You have somewhat of an advantage because the banking rules allow you to loan out about five times the amount you have received in deposits—amazing but true. So if you have a $1,000 deposit that you must pay 3 percent interest or $30 per year, you can loan out $5,000 and charge 6 percent interest or $300 per year. That leaves you $270 to pay those employees and advertising companies. If you do it right, you'll even have a little left over to pay your stockholders a dividend.

What if you loan out the $5,000 and never get it back? Oops. That isn't supposed to happen. Your *credit analysis* of that borrower convinced you he was likely to pay it back. Now you need to take that $270 from other loans that are repaid and repay the loan yourself. Eventually, you'll separate borrowers into different risk categories and charge the riskier ones higher interest rates so that it will take fewer of them to repay the bad loans. Competition for the less risky folks will force you to charge them increasingly lower interest rates to keep their business. It is a very responsive market with enough players that the interest rates respond very quickly to supply and demand.

def•i•ni•tion

A **credit analysis** is the process a creditor uses to decide which consumers to do business with.

Different lenders specialize in different types of loans. They also look for different characteristics in their customers. You may look like a potential candidate to borrow money to buy a house and still not qualify for a car loan. Let's go through the most common types of credit and find out what might impact a lender's decision to do business with you.

Mortgages

One thing that greatly reduces the risk of doing business with people is the practice of pledging an asset to back a loan if the loan is not repaid. This asset is called collateral. The borrower signs a mortgage or a lien pledging that asset to back the loan. With real estate mortgages, another even more startling thing reduces the risk to the lender: people can't move the real estate. Everyone will always know where it is! It is true that the structures on it can be damaged, but the land isn't going anywhere.

For residential real estate loans, the lender has another bonus: he can usually find the borrower, too, because the borrower will probably be living on the real estate while he is repaying the debt. If the lender must take action to collect the debt, finding the borrower and finding the collateral are two key issues that make this job much easier.

Most mortgage loans require an amount of money down on the purchase of the property, which leaves the collateral valued at more than the amount of the loans. This reduces the risk to the lender that a decrease in the value of the property will mean the lender can't recover the entire amount of the loan if he has to seize the asset.

Because of these and other ways to reduce the risk they are taking, lenders can charge lower interest rates and do business with people who have a less than stellar credit history. Homeownership has been a cornerstone of our economy's success, and many government programs reduce the risk to the lenders by guaranteeing the loans as well.

Credit Cautions

Don't manage your personal financial decisions around the notion that having a moderate amount of outstanding debt looks good to future creditors. If you can live debt-free, do so, and only do business with companies that respect you for your superior money-management skills.

Car Loans

Unlike homes, cars can be moved—and the debtors can move around with them. Also unlike homes, cars decrease in value the moment you drive them off the lot. Many loan offers require little or nothing down, increasing the risk to the lender. But the market for money to buy cars is huge, and car manufacturers figured out years ago they could probably turn a bigger profit selling the money than selling the cars.

Consumers kept demanding lower down payments and longer loan repayment periods, increasing the risk to the lenders even more. The cars would be worth much less than the loan balance when they were traded in, so the balance would be rolled over to the new loan. This situation put both the creditor and the debtor at greater risk.

Creditors began minimizing their risk by doing business with only very creditworthy people. Car loans were about the most difficult loan to get if you had any dings on your credit report. This reality fueled the "buy here, pay here" industry: car dealers who finance their own vehicles by jacking up the sales prices and taking weekly installment payments.

To Your Credit

Credit.About (www.credit.about.com) is an interactive, educational, and informational site designed to help consumers learn about credit and debt.

The other response to this market was to not actually sell the cars but to rent them for extended periods. Leasing has become popular because consumers want to drive cars they can't afford. The leasing company, often a subsidiary of the manufacturer, charges a monthly amount for the use of the vehicle up to a certain number of miles. The consumer then returns the car at the end of the rental period and pays for any extra mileage or damage incurred.

Credit Cards

Charge cards started gaining popularity in the 1960s. Master Charge and Bank Americard (now known as MasterCard and Visa, respectively) developed networks of banks and *agent banks* across the country to allow their customers to have one account to use at all the stores. Initially, the department stores that had their own charge cards didn't accept the bank cards. But they slowly changed their credit agreements to look more like the bank cards, charging interest and allowing less than the full balance to be paid each month.

def•i•ni•tion

> **Agent banks** are smaller banks that serve as representatives for larger banks in credit card services.

Consumer Loans

As creditors became more sophisticated in their credit-analysis skills and the credit-reporting agencies became more reliable in reporting an accurate picture of a potential debtor, the industry began to segment. Lower-risk borrowers continued to find favorable interest rates at banks and savings and loans. Higher-risk borrowers migrated to new firms called finance companies. These were mostly subsidiaries of banks, designed to attract and serve higher-risk borrowers with higher-interest, lower-balance loans. They normally bump up their interest rates to the maximum allowed by the law.

They were successful at financing consumer products that might be too expensive for a normal credit card limit, such as appliances or home furnishings. They began the "90 days same as cash" marketing gimmick to attract people by promising no interest for a certain period of time.

Another marketing ploy was to send out checks for $500 loans that the consumer could just cash to go into debt, a practice that has been regulated in many places as an unfair practice. The entire check-cashing industry then stepped in to do the smaller, usurious loans, preying on people with no hope of qualifying for low-interest credit. Interest rates soared to over 300 percent on these loans. That industry is now coming under stricter regulations in many states, but no doubt another industry will spring up to service this always-present market.

To Your Credit

Same-as-cash loans from retailers seem like a very smart consumer move, but they can quickly turn sour on a credit report. They are issued not by the retailer but by third-party consumer finance companies offering the highest interest rates allowed in your state. If you miss the same-as-cash deadline, these interest fees can add up quickly. They also raise eyebrows with more legitimate lenders when you are looking for low-interest loans.

Measurements of Creditworthiness

Your credit report summarizes your past behavior with credit contracts you have signed. It also indicates how much available credit you have that you aren't currently using. It lists other facts, including your address and employer, but it doesn't give your entire financial picture. Other facts about you are very important to creditors when determining your creditworthiness, so let's review some of the most important ones.

Account History

Each credit reference on your credit report indicates the historical manner in which you have managed the payments on your account and might indicate the balance fluctuations on a revolving charge. It will tell your highest balance, or initial loan value, and your current balance.

These factors comprise the biggest part of your credit score. Recent late payments will negatively impact your score, and account balances near the credit limits will also bring your score down.

Income vs. Expenses

As a financial counselor, I often met with people recently turned down for a new credit account. They were confused and upset because they had what they thought was a perfect credit report. They'd never been late on anything! After adding up their debt, we usually found that their total amount owed equaled half of their annual income, making their debt-to-income ratio 50 percent. It seemed that, at that point, the creditors didn't believe they had enough cash left to service any new debt obligations each month.

Let's say that a family with $80,000 income, or $4,500 per month after taxes, was $40,000 in debt. Those payments would be around $1,000 a month, more than 20 percent of the monthly income. This is where the creditors seemed to pull the plug. It's unfortunate these families didn't see any warning signs before the creditors cut them off. As long as the payments were in on time and the cards were still usable, they didn't think they had a problem.

Even though your income is not a factor in your credit score calculation, you still need to prove the capacity to repay the debt you are incurring. You need to prove this to yourself through careful planning and budgeting before you set out to prove it to a creditor. Don't think that a creditor who doesn't take your income into account is doing you a favor by approving a credit line you can't afford to repay.

To Your Credit

Instead of jumping on the first lower-interest credit card offer that comes in the mail, call your current company and ask it to match the lower rate. That will make one fewer account you'll need to manage on your credit report, and you won't be labeled a credit jumper, someone who moves frequently from account to account.

The same happens with mortgages. Mortgage companies, which are in the business of selling you a bigger mortgage, will loan you much more money than your cash flow can afford. Only you really know what you prefer to spend money on.

Net Worth

Your net worth is the difference between what you own and what you owe. If you are a 20-year-old with a car worth $10,000, a car loan balance of $12,000, and a credit card balance of $3,000, you have a net worth of –$5,000. If you are a retired worker with a home worth $200,000, a mortgage of $20,000, and a retirement account worth $300,000, your net worth is $480,000. This number is a snapshot of your financial well-being and, when considered with other facts about you, can help a financial institution decide whether you are a good prospect for credit.

Along with managing your creditworthiness, paying attention to your net worth is a solid financial-planning strategy that can help guide you to good credit decisions. If you are entering into debt to purchase something that will increase your net worth in the long run, such as a home or more education, it is probably a good decision.

No Such Thing as "Perfect Credit"

By now you might have figured out that, just like beauty, credit is in the eye of the beholder. Your particular situation might look very attractive to one lender for a particular type of loan and very unattractive to a different lender for a different type of loan. You might pay off your credit card every month in full on time, thinking that this makes your credit look great. But a credit card company makes its living off folks who incur interest and late fees. It doesn't particularly want your business.

You might be carrying around a bankruptcy filing on your credit report thinking you could never get a mortgage, but some mortgage lenders lend only to people with damaged credit.

Your credit will be perfect when it allows you to reach your own financial goals. If you want to be a real estate investor, you'll want to build a very different credit report than someone who is investing everything in mutual funds. Figure out where you want to be financially, and build the report that will get you there.

The Least You Need to Know

- Trust is a highly studied phenomenon that leads to highly efficient credit markets.

- Your trustworthiness or creditworthiness is measured in several ways, including widely used credit scores.

- Your creditworthiness is directly tied to what price you pay to borrow money.

- Becoming an undesirable customer to one type of lender makes you attractive to another type.

What Is Debt?

In This Chapter

- Distinguishing between credit and debt
- Understanding good debt and bad debt
- Determining your financial position

When you pay cash for something, you're using money you've already earned. When you put something on a credit card, you are promising to pay with either money you already have in the bank or money you haven't earned yet. Your credit is the amount of future earnings someone would let you spend today. Your debt is the amount of future earnings you have already spent.

When Credit Leads to Debt

It's a nice sense of security to know you can get a cash advance in a hurry if you have needs today greater than your current resources can handle. But it's a bad sign when you begin to rely only on that credit for unforeseen needs. Your savings program should include short-term, midterm, and long-term needs. Many workers in the United States have only long-term tax-deferred savings through their 401(k) programs. When they have a midterm crisis, such as a car repair, they turn to credit cards, consumer loans, or 401(k) loans to finance it, and these payments further erode their ability to save for ongoing needs. The cycle continues, leading to even more debt.

When Debt Leads to No Credit

At some point, the debt load can become burdensome enough that lenders won't allow you to finance the next midterm crisis. This means you'll have to pay for the crisis with cash you should be using to make debt payments that month. Late payments on loans and credit cards ding the credit report, warning future creditors that you are not reliable anymore. The load can also become high enough to kick you out of reasonable debt-to-income ratios.

Similarly, if you lose your job during a time when every penny of your budget goes to paying the debts on time, payments will become late. Having a great deal of debt makes your creditworthiness vulnerable to a range of difficulties.

To Your Credit

Many young people think of their first credit card as additional income or money they have to spend. In fact, it is just the opposite. It will take money out of their cash flow as they repay the interest on those purchases over time.

Available Credit Is Not Debt

Because a person's creditworthiness might drop at the exact moment he needs ready cash, more people are opening equity lines of credit or applying for low-fee credit cards but using them only in a true crisis. This available credit is not debt under our previous definition. It can be a wonderful strategy, as long as you dip into the money only during a crisis.

The Difference Between a Credit Report and Creditworthiness

Your credit report can say many things about you— some true, some not. It can reflect the behavior of an ex-spouse. It can expose a fraud perpetrated on you. It can speak to a medical crisis you suffered five years ago and have fully recovered from. It might or might not reflect your true creditworthiness.

The purpose of this book is to help you bring your state of creditworthiness and your credit report into alignment. If you are a totally creditworthy person although your report says something different, you can change that. If you are not behaving in a credit-worthy manner, you can change that, too, and your report will reflect that change. It is important that you understand the difference between your cred-itworthiness and your credit report as you develop your ongoing strategy to manage both.

The Difference Between Good and Bad Debt

Our economy is fueled by debt. All governments operate by issuing bonds. All major corporations acquire assets and expand markets by using debt. Almost every homeowner starts out in a lot of debt. It's what we do.

But somewhere along the way, we lost the distinc-tion between good and bad debt. Good debt allows us to build our net worth and become financially secure. Bad debt puts us in jeopardy of losing every-thing and having to start building our net worth all over again. Lenders have spent millions advertis-ing the advantages of debt to finance vacations and meals out (expenses) or cars and furniture (depreci-ating assets), leaving us confused about the best uses of debt. So let me sort this out for you.

Debt Backing Appreciating Assets

Debt can be a very good thing when a person uses it to purchase assets that increase in value. To give you an idea of what I'm talking about, consider the following example. Your kid comes to you one summer day and says, "I'd like to put up a lemonade stand today, but I don't have any lemonade." You run to the store and spend $5 on lemonade powder, $1 on paper cups, and $2 on ice. You tell him he can keep half of anything over the $8 investment. You drive a hard bargain. By the end of the day, he counts all the quarters and wrinkled dollars: $14.50. He made $3.25 and learned about the cost of capital. You earned a 14,600 percent return on your money (*APR*) and decided you could retire if you moved to a warmer climate.

def•i•ni•tion

The **APR**, or **annual percentage rate**, is the interest paid on a loan, calculated on a yearly basis. It might be higher than the stated interest rate because interest is compounded (charged on interest already incurred). According to the Federal Truth in Lending Act, every consumer loan agreement must disclose the APR in large bold type.

What really happened here is that your child went into debt to finance his inventory and was able to use this investment in his business to make a profit.

He added his own time, some presentation, and salesmanship to increase the value of his inventory from $8 to $14.50.

Student Loans

If you consider humans and their earning potential as increasing assets, then education is the commodity that increases their value. If a high school graduate in your community can find work at $8 per hour and a college grad can find work at $15 per hour, the value of the education can be measured as the return on the investment in the tuition. Going into debt to finance this investment can make a lot of financial sense if there is no other alternative. Students make these decisions intuitively, knowing that their lives and their opportunities will be much different with the more education they complete.

With soaring tuition costs, some students are wisely looking at the relative earning potential of graduates of different degree programs or colleges before they calculate how much debt they are willing to absorb. Even doctors, who have historically high earning rates, are often finding it difficult to shoulder the student loan debt they leave school with. Since student loans have deferred payment schedules, they can seem affordable at first. But when the payment books finally arrive as the student is just starting a career, they can quickly cause financial hardship.

> ### Credit Cautions
>
> Credit insurance purchased to ensure the payment of a credit card balance in the event of death, disability, or unemployment is not just too expensive. When the premium is added to the interest on some cards, it exceeds the minimum payment, so it puts you in more debt each month!

Mortgages

Since the Great Depression, only recently have we seen real estate prices decline in some areas of the country. For the most part, residential real estate has been a solid investment, and using debt to buy it has been a sound financial decision. The government has even encouraged this strategy by excluding the interest paid on mortgage debt from income taxation.

Historically, most mortgage lenders have required 5 or 10 percent down on the property, leaving some leeway for the need to sell it quickly and the cost of selling it with a real estate agent. But recently we have seen loans which have allowed individuals to be upside down on their mortgage, owing more than the home is worth. This happens in a few different ways: (1) a second mortgage is issued for more than the value of the home, (2) the home value actually declines, or (3) the home is sold quickly for less than it is worth and the balance is rolled into a mortgage for a new property. This unsecured portion of the mortgage can leave the homeowner in a risky situation just as other unsecured debt might.

To Your Credit

Lenders (especially mortgage lenders) banter around ratios and percentages that prescribe good amounts of debt to not exceed. These limits are for their marketing and underwriting use and are much too high for most households to manage well. Do your own budget to see how much debt you can repay. Don't believe their numbers.

The sub-prime mortgage crisis of 2008 is an example of how mortgage lenders were able to talk potential homeowners into debt they could not reasonably afford to repay. In many cases, they fiddled with credit scores so people could qualify. They also structured loans with lower payments in early years, giving borrowers a false sense of affordability. Even with this terrible track record, nothing will prevent them from continuing to use marketing strategies that trick you into buying a bigger house than you can afford or entering into mortgage debt that is beyond your capacity to repay. Remember that your mortgage loan officer is not your financial planner. Do your own calculations and seek other advice if you are unsure.

Consumer Debt

Let's say you buy a big-screen TV with your Sears credit card for $2,000 and make the minimum payments on the credit card until you pay it off. That TV cost you more than $7,000. Sears might have made $1,000 by selling you the TV, but it made $5,000 by selling you the money. It makes you wonder what business it is in.

Marketing experts know you will spend more on any given shopping trip if you intend to use a credit card than if you have a specific amount of cash with you. They offer in-store discounts on your purchases today, in exchange for opening an account at their store. They know they'll quickly earn back what they've given up.

It's convenient to not have to carry large sums of cash. It's nice to get a record of your purchases. It's very nice to be able to challenge a purchase or receive insurance on it because you used a credit card. And it's great to get cash back or bonus airline mileage for using a card. But if all these incentives cause you to spend more than you would have, you need to consider the real costs to your financial position.

Predatory Lenders

The increasing efficiency of our credit-reporting systems in this country has disqualified a huge segment of the population from receiving loans. Most dings follow you for seven years, but life goes on, and some needs are beyond this week's paycheck. In response, a new set of lenders has evolved to service this population. The Federal Reserve Bank calls them predatory lenders.

The notion is that they prey on the financially weak. Some of them might not even look like lenders to the uninformed. Rent-to-own retailers; buy-here, pay-here car lots; check-cashing firms; and pawn shops are among the types of firms that depend on customers with bad credit. Effective annual percentage rates at these companies soar into the triple digits. The consumers have no other choice to meet their needs and willingly use their services. Once they are caught in this web of high fees and weekly payments, it is difficult to wiggle free.

Your Financial Position

You are where you are. Any decisions you have made up to this point are made. You won't be changing them, but it is helpful to understand what effect they have had on your financial position and whether you want to make different decisions from this point forward. To do that, you start by adding up where you are. These common financial statements are a good place to start:

- A balance sheet
- An income statement

Let's look at each in turn.

Balance Sheets: Assets vs. Liabilities

A balance sheet is a list of your assets (what you own) compared to your liabilities (what you owe) and your net worth (the difference between the two). Make a list of your assets and your liabilities, and look up the current value of each item on the list. Use the current market value to give you a realistic picture. You can guess the value of your home by looking at recent sales in your neighborhood of similar homes. You can get your car's current value in the *Kelley Blue Book*. You should value other jewelry and household goods at about half of what you would pay for them today. Any investment accounts can be valued by your last statements from them. Liabilities are the amount you need to pay off the loans or accounts in full today.

This quick snapshot tells you your financial strength if you were to liquidate everything today. If you owe more than you own, you are technically bankrupt, even though you aren't filing bankruptcy. You'll want to turn those numbers around as quickly as possible. If you have a positive net worth, you want to develop strategies to both protect and grow it. Think about how losses in income or casualty losses would affect your net worth. Review your entire insurance portfolio to make sure you don't have any gaps you can't afford.

Income Statements: Income vs. Expenses

An income statement is a way to peek at your financial situation to see if your cash flow is positive or negative. Everything coming in minus everything going out is your cash flow. If this number is negative, it means you are going into debt and reducing your net worth each month. If it is positive, it means you are adding to your asset base and increasing your net worth each month.

For most households, this is a difficult report to compile as you must capture many different income sources and expenses. You might need to start with what you think the situation is and then track it for a couple of months, adjusting your income statement as you go. The goal is to arrive at a positive cash flow that will add to your net worth on your balance sheet each month.

There is one complicated notion in compiling these two reports. Money that you pay down on the principal of loans or credit cards is not an expense on the income statement, but the interest is. Money that you send to investment accounts or pay toward the equity of your home isn't an expense, either. Since both of these transactions directly increase your net worth, they are applied directly to your balance sheet.

The Least You Need to Know

- Debt can be a wonderful financial tool when used to finance appreciating assets.
- Many consumers confuse the convenience of credit cards with the sources of real cash in their financial lives.

- Even mortgages can become bad debt when used to finance more than the value of the home.

- Knowing your net worth and tracking it as a measurement of your financial well-being is a great place to start.

Chapter 5

The Anatomy of a Credit Report

In This Chapter

- The different types of credit-reporting companies
- Getting your reports
- Reading your reports

When I was a financial counselor, my clients often asked me if I could pull their credit reports for them. I once asked the local credit bureau how that would work. Reading through the fine print of the membership agreement, I noticed it stated that I would have to report the credit experience I had with my customers. I wanted no part of that, but it made sense that the system couldn't work any other way. If everyone wanted only to read other credit references but never report his own, who would there be to send in their experiences with you as a creditor?

The Credit-Reporting Industry

The practice of compiling credit reports has grown through encouraging the regular voluntary submission of timely data. *Credit bureau members* submit information on their customers. The credit-reporting agencies don't pay for this information (and may even charge), so in a sense, their stock in trade is free to them.

def•i•ni•tion

> **Credit bureau members** or subscribers are the businesses that pay a fee to belong to or do business with the credit bureaus and, therefore, can order consumer reports from them. They decide whether to grant credit based on the information provided.

You probably want to become familiar with five major national players. The Big Three are Equifax, Experian, and TransUnion. These companies also own subsidiaries that collect a variety of information. An example is the Medical Information Bureau (MIB) owned by Equifax. The fourth company is ChexSystems, a subsidiary of Deluxe Check Printers, which collects only information relative to the handling of bank accounts and ATM/debit cards. Dun and Bradstreet is the leading player in collecting credit information on businesses.

Credit Cautions

Another company, Innovis, has become a national player, but its business is currently confined to selling mailing lists based on credit-selection criteria. You can order your report from them by calling 1-800-540-2505, but you might not want to correct any negative information on it. You might just see more junk mail in your mailbox. You can opt out of preapproved credit offers at www.optoutprescreen.com.

Companies That Sell You Information

You have the right to view the files the Big Three keep on you. You can request copies of your consumer files at a cost that your state mandates. In addition, a federal law called the FACT Act (see Chapter 12) requires credit companies to provide a yearly free report to all who ask. ChexSystems reports are free as well. You are also entitled to free reports if you have recently been declined credit, insurance, or employment; if you are unemployed and seeking work; if you are receiving government assistance; if you have been the victim of fraud; or if you have requested a correction to your report.

Numerous companies resell your credit information, with many combining all three reports into a single, more readable format. Some of these companies will advertise a free report but have you enroll in their credit-monitoring service. A search on the Internet for *credit reports* will yield dozens of such companies. Ordering a combined report from a reseller can sometimes be confusing, especially if you discover errors. You might be surprised at how each report can differ from the others.

To Your Credit

If you haven't seen your reports in the last year, order the reports from each of the Big Three (Experian, Equifax, and TransUnion) at www.annualcreditreport. com or by calling 1-877-322-8228.

Companies That Notify You of Changes to Your Report

We've all received offers to get a free look at our credit reports. All we have to do is sign up for a credit-monitoring service—money back if we're not satisfied. These services will send you an alert each time someone pulls your report or adds new information. You'll also receive a notice from them anytime a derogatory mark ends up on your report. If your reports are just the way you want them and you want to protect yourself from errors, fraud, and illegal inquiries, these services are likely a better value than ordering your report several times a year yourself. Each of the Big Three offers these services, as do other independent firms, so if this sounds good to you, shop around and check out the firms before you sign up.

A recent player in this business is the company that calculates credit scores, Fair Isaac. They have a range of monitoring services that also includes giving you an updated credit score periodically. Some of their customers, banks and credit card companies, are now automatically including your FICO score on each statement you receive from them. If you have or can open an account with one of these institutions, you can watch your score to check for any negative impact for free.

To Your Credit

Look at the inquiries on your report carefully. Who is accessing your report, and do you know them? They must have a business reason or legitimate purpose. In many cases, they need your signed permission. Your report is private and can be shared only with those you choose to do business with.

How to Get Your Reports

You are entitled to one free report from each of the three national agencies each year. You don't have to order them all at one time, so you can look at one every four months, which is a nice strategy. You can only get the free reports through this clearinghouse:

Annual Credit Report Request Service
1-877-322-8228 (1-877-FACTACT)
PO Box 105281
Atlanta, GA 30374-5281
www.annualcreditreport.com

Here are the three national credit-reporting agencies and how to contact them for your second report or other free reports in any given year:

Equifax
1-800-685-1111
PO Box 740241
Atlanta, GA 30374
www.equifax.com

Experian
1-888-Experian (1-888-397-3742)
PO Box 2104
Allen, TX 75013
www.experian.com

TransUnion
1-800-888-4213
PO Box 1000
Chester, PA 19022
www.transunion.com

Writing

Mailing in a request for reports used to be the only way to access them. It's not the most popular method today, but you can still do it this way. You need to include two forms of identification and wait a couple of weeks for the report. They also need your Social Security number, full name, and current and previous addresses. Even though you can now call or order reports online from the other companies, some people prefer to write because they like to keep copies of their correspondence and receipts for mailing. If you order your report online, you may still be required to mail in identifying information.

Each company has different requirements to identify you and mail you a report. The first issue is that
they'll only send the report to the address on the
report, so if that is wrong, you'll need to send in
proof of your new address.

Calling

If you'd like to buy a report or are entitled to a
free report for reasons other than your FACT Act
annual report, you can call each of the companies and ask them to send the report in the mail.
All three companies will *sell* you reports over the
phone. As you can imagine, you must negotiate a
series of phone prompts to enter the information
and identify yourself.

Internet Sources

Each company has an interactive, comprehensive
website where you can order a report. Ordering a
report online has the advantage of instant delivery.
They also allow online corrections and challenges
to the information in the report.

To Your Credit _____

Schedule the day each year you review
your credit report by linking it with something else that happens automatically,
such as the notice from your dentist to
have your teeth cleaned or your tax return
filing deadline. It's just about as much fun
as both of those events!

To provide customers with immediate access online while ensuring everyone's privacy, the credit companies must take reasonable precautions so as not to release the information to the wrong people. Be prepared to verify information on your report, such as what kind of car you financed last year or how much your mortgage payment is. The problem with this system is that you might not know the answers to the questions, especially if the credit-report file is incorrect. With Experian, if you answer a question incorrectly, you are prevented from trying again for a week. With the others, you can call a toll-free number provided and verify your identity over the phone.

How to Read Your Reports

With the introduction of online reports, all three reports have become much more readable. Gone are the cryptic, almost secret, codes that could make your eyes glaze over. Most information is now in words, not symbols or numbers. The only hard part is figuring out what is missing since they no longer use standardized fields. You can easily see this on a combined report, where the information is side-by-side in three columns.

Information Included in Reports

The main sections of the credit report are as follows:

- **Summary**—The number of potentially negative items (dings) on the report and the accounts in good standing

- **Personal Information**—Social Security number variations, date of birth, driver's license number, telephone numbers, spouse's first name, and employers

- **Public Records**—The court and case number, location number, date filed, date resolved, responsibility, claim amount and liability amount, and other status details

- **Collection Agency Information**—Name of collector, original creditor (client), original amount, state, balance, ownership, account number

- **Credit Account Information**—Company, shortened account number, date opened, highest balance, credit limit, terms, months reviewed, date reported, balance, past due amount, last pay date, last amount paid, scheduled payment amount, most recent activity, date of last activity, date of first major delinquency, amount charged off, and date account closed

- **Your Use of Credit**—Additional information on some accounts, showing up to 24 months of balance history and your credit limit

- **Inquiries That Display to Companies**—All authorized and other legitimate requests to view your credit file

- **Requests Viewed Only by You**—Inquiries from creditors offering you preapproved credit, potential employers, potential investors, and current creditors monitoring your accounts

- **Consumer Statements**—Statements you
  have added to the report to explain any
  information you believe is incorrect or mis-
  leading
- **Addresses of Creditors (online only)**—
  Creditor addresses so you can correspond
  directly with the creditor

Credit Cautions

A credit line, line of credit, or credit
limit is the amount of total debt you
can incur on a revolving credit account.
Some creditors might not grant you new
credit if you have a large credit limit
on existing accounts because it is readily available to you, even if you haven't
tapped into it. The irony of this is that the
FICO score actually increases as your percentage of outstanding balances to credit
limits decreases, so having untapped
credit (if it isn't too much compared to your
income) can help you.

Combined Reports

Combined reports are available online. They pull
data from all three reporting agencies into a single
report. Many combined reports list data in three
columns, one for each of the agencies. The data is
formatted differently than it is on the three credit
companies' reports.

Such reports are useful because they allow you to look at the data side-by-side to determine whether any of the credit companies are missing or misreporting data. If you are about to apply for credit, you cannot be sure which agency will be selling the data to your potential creditor, so combined reports make it easy for you to look at them all. If you ask the company providing the combined report to investigate an incorrect item, the originating agency will send you a corrected report, so you can see the individual report as well.

Credit Scoring

Nothing is quite as annoying as reducing your whole existence to a single number. Your SAT score, your weight, your cholesterol, the number of days since you've had sex—one number can never really capture the real you. But the credit scorers think they can come close. A business called the Fair Isaacs Company has combined just about everything quantifiable about your creditworthiness into a single number, called your FICO score.

Your FICO score is an objective method credit grantors use to determine how much, if any, credit to grant to an applicant. Some of the factors used in creating the score are income, assets, length of employment, length of living in one place, and past responsibility with using credit.

To Your Credit

The Credit Info Center, at www.creditinfocenter.com, is a site that challenges the Big Three credit-reporting agencies, credit-counseling firms, and other anti-consumer organizations, providing opinions and links to resources.

Scores range from about 300 to 850 and fluctuate every time something changes in your credit situation. Most picky creditors consider a score higher than 740 a good score. You can obtain your scores online at www.myfico.com for a small fee. You will receive three scores because Fair Isaacs Company calculates scores based on the information contained in each of your three credit reports. Because the three agencies don't have the same information, the scores might be different but should be somewhat close. If they're not, it could be a sign that one or more of your reports contain inaccuracies.

Creditors don't use FICO scores just to approve or decline credit. They also sometimes use them to determine what interest rate to offer. A drop of 50 points in your FICO might mean an extra half point on a mortgage loan.

Take Action Now!

You'll never know what your credit reports say about you until you access them, so order your three reports and your credit score today. Then use the information contained in this chapter to read and review them.

The Least You Need to Know

- The three major credit-reporting agencies each compile a report on your credit history; potential creditors can access these reports to check you out.

- The three credit-reporting agencies don't share information with each other and don't make credit-granting decisions.

- You can get your reports anytime you want, either electronically or through the mail.

- Your credit score reduces the information on your three reports to three distinct numbers.

Chapter 6

All About Dings

In This Chapter

- Identifying the negative items on your report
- How a bad item makes it to your report and how long it stays there
- The impact inquiries have on your report

Creditors look at a variety of indicators when evaluating your credit report, many of which are now rolled into the automatic calculations that create credit scores. Understanding each of these items that negatively impact your report and your score is the key to maintaining a good report.

Late Payments

"Late" means different things to different people. Some people pay their bills the day they get them; some pay them on the next payday. Some pay them as close to the due date as possible, and some pay them only when a late fee or other consequence is looming.

Then the creditors complicate the matter with grace periods. Many homeowners begin to believe their mortgage payment is due on the 15th because the late fee is assessed on the 16th. This is not true. The payment is due on the 1st, even though there is a 15-day grace period during which no late fee is charged.

Credit-reporting agencies normally collect data on how many times you have been 30 days, 60 days, and 90 days late with a payment. So you could have paid the late fee every month of your loan, but if you paid it before 30 days, your credit report will still be clean.

> **To Your Credit**
>
> Late payment information can stay on your report for up to seven years. But if the account is still open and active, that company might report only the last three to four years, so the old negative activity will cycle off much faster. Your report indicates how many months each credit reference reports. Paying off these accounts early might actually *hurt* your credit, amazingly, by freezing those late payment references on the report.

Excessive Debt

A couple came to see me in my financial-counseling practice one evening. Both were under obvious stress. He looked at her and said, "I really don't see what the problem is. We always pay our bills on time. We have great credit." She just sighed, looked at me, and said, "You'll see." As we opened one envelope after another, my spreadsheet grew and grew. By the time we were done, the screen said $123,500 in unsecured debt. This was not counting the $200,000 mortgage and a couple of cars.

He was right: their income of $170,000 a year was plenty to make the minimum payments, but they were incurring close to $20,000 in interest charges. All their accounts were maxed out, and they had no money in the bank other than their last paycheck.

Debts can be good or bad, in the creditor's eyes. But even good debts can keep you from qualifying for new loans or credit accounts. When you are beyond the point at which a creditor can see enough income to service all your debts well, you will be declined for new debt.

To Your Credit

When a report has a ding, or a bad mark, people tend to adopt the attitude that anything else bad on the report can't hurt it anymore. This is totally untrue. Each ding takes time to explain, remove, or live with. The more dings you have, the less chance you will have of securing credit in the near future.

Collection Activity

After a certain number of days without sufficient payments, the collections department at your creditor will begin to contact you. Letters and phone calls will remind you how behind you are. They will explain consequences and offer suggestions to get caught up. Many times they will propose an amnesty program that allows you to make a certain number of payments on time, which will erase all past-due balances. Sometimes these programs, known as re-aging, can impact your credit report very favorably.

> **Credit Cautions**
>
> The true cost of a bad credit report is in the increased interest rates that you might incur on future mortgages and car loans. Walking away from a $5,000 debt through bankruptcy or other means might seem like you saved some money, but it could cost you tens of thousands over the following several years in higher-interest loans.

Eventually, the creditor *charges off* the debt and sends it to a collection agency. These are separate companies that work for more than one creditor and make money by recovering bad debts for those creditors. If your account has been turned over to a collection agency, the agency will send you an introductory letter explaining that the account has been placed with them for collection. In addition, the agency usually demands the balance in full within a certain number of days.

At this point, your credit report will reflect two things. First, the account will show the status as a 9, the worst rating a debt can have (see Chapter 5). Second, there will be a listing in the collection activity section showing who is collecting the debt. Both of these references will be very damaging to your credit score and your creditworthiness. After you pay off the debt and some time has passed, some potential creditors will downgrade their importance when considering you for new loans, but the reference will remain on your report for seven years.

def•i•ni•tion

The creditor **charges off** a debt when it declares a debt uncollectable. This action allows the creditor to expense the balance as a loss for business and tax purposes. You might receive a 1099 at tax time declaring the amount charged off as income to you. If so, you will need to include it on your 1040 and pay the taxes on it.

Judgments, Liens, and Bankruptcy

If the collection agency is unsuccessful in collecting the debt within a reasonable time frame, the agency might recommend to the creditor that it obtain a *judgment* in a local court.

def•i•ni•tion

A civil **judgment** is a decision by a court that a debt is owed and an order is issued to pay the debt to the creditor. It is enforceable by certain actions, such as garnishment of assets and wages in some states.

When a creditor obtains a judgment, the legal notice will appear on your credit report. It should also indicate whether it has been satisfied or settled. A satisfied judgment is one paid in full per the court order. A settled judgment is one in which the creditor has agreed to take less than the court ordered to be paid. Be aware that some loans, known as cognovit loans, allow the creditor to receive a judgment without your knowledge. Be very careful if you have signed this type of agreement.

Liens filed in court can also appear on your credit report. When a situation has reached the point that judgments and liens are being threatened, many debtors turn to the bankruptcy court for protection of their assets and wages. When a bankruptcy is complete, the debts included in the filing no longer show a balance due on the credit report. The *reaffirmed* debts continue to be reported normally. The filing itself appears on the report under the section with the legal notices. A Chapter 13 remains for 7 years; a Chapter 7 remains for 10 years.

def•i•ni•tion

Reaffirmation is the exclusion of a debt from a bankruptcy process, promising to pay the debt in full after the bankruptcy.

Excessive Inquiries

The inquiry section of your credit report lets a potential creditor ask, "What's wrong with this picture?" For example, if there is an inquiry from Citibank but no corresponding debt listed, it could mean one of four things: Citibank pulled this report illegally; you applied to Citibank for credit, but Citibank turned you down; you applied to Citibank for credit, but you turned it down; or you just accepted credit from Citibank, and it hasn't shown up yet.

All but the first of these possible scenarios is troublesome to a potential creditor. Why did Citibank turn you down? What might Citibank know about you that you haven't disclosed to this creditor? If you turned down Citibank, are you just looking and not a serious shopper? And if you have just accepted a new credit account, how much is it?

You can have a good number of inquiries, as long as they make sense. Creditors routinely pull reports on their customers to look for signs of trouble elsewhere. All creditors pull reports before accounts are opened, except on their most trusted customers.

Credit Cautions

In the past, if you were shopping for a car and in one day six car dealers ran your credit report, those inquiries would have counted against you as excessive. New federal laws prohibit such discrimination. So shop as much as you need to find the best deal.

The Least You Need to Know

- If you are falling behind in your payments, try to keep everything less than 30 days late instead of keeping some perfectly on time and letting others fall 60 or 90 days late.

- Remember that your total debt load can be just as damaging to your report as a handful of late payment histories.

- All public records and court activity will be reflected on your reports.

- Inquiries are not as damaging as they used to be, but it is still prudent to avoid applying for credit carelessly.

Making Changes to Your Credit Report

In This Chapter

- Disputing mistakes on your report
- Negotiating with creditors for a better report
- Fooling credit bureaus—it rarely works
- Building your report with nonreporting creditors

Under the law, it's your right to have accurate information on your credit reports. It's your responsibility, however, to notice when it's inaccurate. Fortunately, in recent years, federal legislation and improvements in data processing have streamlined the investigation process.

Disputing Mistakes

In the following sections, I walk you through the steps involved in disputing errors with various institutions. I also offer some tips for getting negative but accurate information changed.

With the Reporting Agencies

When you receive a written copy of your report, it might come with a form you can use to dispute a claim made on it. When you have the forms, the process of filling them out is straightforward. However, before you fill out any of these forms, I encourage you to make multiple copies because they don't have room for many disputes. I also suggest copying the credit report, highlighting the erroneous information, and sending that along with the form. If you have documentation that can prove the error, send that along as well. Keep copies of *everything* you send.

If you ordered your report online, requesting an investigation is fairly easy. Each agency has an online process to notify it of errors to be investigated. If you ordered your report through a reseller or ordered a combined report, you'll need to get a copy of your actual report from the appropriate agency before you can challenge anything. The agency will need the file number or identifying number printed on the report. So if you are serious about getting all the inaccurate information off your reports and you don't mind paying for the online versions of them, go to each credit-reporting agency's website and order the reports individually. Then you can challenge the report online immediately.

To Your Credit

If you believe your credit report has inaccurate information, give yourself at least a month before you apply for credit, employment, or insurance. This gives you time to view your report and begin correcting any errors or adding consumer statements.

Each form, whether on paper or online, will ask you fairly easy questions to identify yourself and the problem. Be as accurate and complete as possible. Don't give them any reason to ignore your request. The credit agencies are inundated with frivolous requests from the credit-repair industry and so are justifiably suspicious. They also don't accept disputes from third parties without a properly executed power of attorney.

When the credit agencies receive your dispute, they have 30 days to investigate and verify the information or take it off. They are required by law to send you the results of their investigation. If the investigation changes the credit reference, the agencies are required to send corrected reports to you and to creditors who recently ordered your report.

With the Credit Grantor

Even if the credit bureau hasn't made any mistakes, your credit report still might contain errors received from your creditors. Asking the credit bureau to verify this kind of information will yield no change in your report. If this happens, it's up to you to convince your creditors that they've made a mistake.

Let's say you've asked for an account to be closed, but it's still reported as open. If the creditor never closed the account, the credit bureau isn't going to be much help. You'll need to continue to work directly with the creditor to get the account closed and to have this reported to the credit bureau.

If time is of the essence, you can request a letter from the creditor and deliver it to the credit bureau independently of the normal process that would update your report.

Negotiating With Creditors

Your creditors are just companies trying to make a profit. Stockholders, regulators, and consumer watchdogs are all standing on the sidelines hoping they'll behave properly. Negotiating with them on the following issues will be more successful if you keep their needs in mind.

Bargaining With Credit Marks

If you've been in *default* on a loan but are now able to catch up your payments, it's absolutely appropriate to ask your creditors to consider reporting your account as having had no late payments in exchange for paying up. If you are paying off a very old debt, you could ask the creditor to completely eliminate it from your report. Of course, the creditor has the right to refuse such requests, but it costs nothing to ask. Your creditors aren't shy about asking you to pay up; you shouldn't be shy about asking them to help you. Nothing in the credit laws requires them to report your history to a credit bureau. Their relationship or contract with a credit-reporting agency might inhibit them from excluding your data, but you can still ask.

def•i•ni•tion

A loan is in **default** when a debtor doesn't make a required payment to the creditor or otherwise violates the terms of the agreement between the creditor and the debtor.

Games People Play

It's human nature to want to hide our faults from view. We created an entire cosmetic industry to make us appear to be people we aren't. When that's not enough, we hire plastic surgeons to make permanent changes. Doctoring our credit reports is simply an extension of this need to have people see what—and only what—we want them to see.

Let's take a look at some of the tricks some have tried to cover credit flaws.

Removing Accurate but Derogatory Information

By law, if you challenge something on your credit report and the credit bureau fails to investigate it or can't confirm the information, the credit bureau has to take it off. The trick some use is to challenge everything, assuming that the bureau will run out of time to verify every item within the 30 days allowed. The laws have reacted, however, to allow the credit bureaus to ignore fallacious disputes. So if you choose to challenge accurate information, be prepared to have all your challenges dismissed as fallacious.

The credit-repair companies count their success by how many bad marks they have removed from your report. The assumption is that these are accurate bad marks because inaccurate bad marks should come off with little effort. So it can and does happen that derogatory information can disappear even though it reflects your actual handling of that account. If you want to play that game, you can try it on your own. If you have only one or two subtle dings, it might make a difference. However, if your report is riddled with collection activity, it's doubtful that this strategy will leave you with a perfectly clean report. In Chapter 10, I explain more about the credit-repair industry and the strategies it uses.

Credit Cautions

Customer service and collection operators at major creditors are usually short-timers and might not have adequate training in how the company's decisions impact your credit report. Always ask to speak to a supervisor when you are looking for help in changing your report.

Changing Identity

Some nefarious credit-repair firms offer to change your identity in an attempt to get out from under a bad credit history by trying to sell you a Credit Privacy Number (CPN) for between $300 and $3,000. They'll claim this number accomplishes the goal of credit file segregation, a process that starts a new credit file for you with new, positive information. It is plainly illegal. Don't try it!

When the Bad Stuff Doesn't Show Up (Lucky You!)

When I worked as a financial counselor, it wasn't unusual to meet people who were so sure their reports had derogatory information that they'd steered their financial plans away from homeownership or other goals that required good credit. When we finally saw the report, however, it was free of dings! Either the creditor they were concerned about never bothered to report the late payment or default or inaccurately reported a good record.

Understandably, people don't usually complain about bad histories that are missing from their reports. And there's no reason they should. It's important to keep in mind, however, that those histories might appear someday if, for instance, the creditor notices that it has the wrong Social Security number for you or discovers some other error that kept the information off your report.

Items Not Normally Reported

You won't see your mother-in-law's name on your report for the money she loaned you for the down payment on the mortgage. Same goes for other personal or family loans—that is, unless Uncle Sal used a collection agency to get his money back from you. Landlords and other small businesses that extend credit, such as florists, orthodontists, and drycleaners, don't normally report either. If you took out a loan or credit card in a business name, it might not show on your report. Utility companies don't normally report unless you enter into a credit agreement with them to purchase equipment or don't pay a final bill. Most aggressive lenders, such as rent-to-own, check-cashing, and pawn shop establishments, also don't report to credit bureaus.

How to Amend Your Report with Nonreporting Creditors

Sometimes it's to your advantage to get some of these nonreporting creditors to report on your payment history. If you're rebuilding a report after a down period, the more positive credit references you have, the better (see Chapter 8). It's within your rights to request that the credit bureau add this reference to your report, but don't be surprised if the bureau charges you a fee for this service if the creditor is not a member of that bureau. See Chapter 13 for a sample letter to get this done.

To Your Credit

If you know you'll be applying for a mortgage in the near future, go ahead and place consumer statements on your reports that point out the errors you have asked to be removed. Most mortgage lenders will merely ask for a written statement from you explaining the dings on your report if they don't disappear in time. These written statements aren't likely to impact your FICO score, however, so they may help you qualify for the loan but might not bring down your interest rate.

Proactive Strategies: Knocking Out the Dings

If you know something unfavorable will be appearing on your report, you can sometimes take steps to minimize the damage it will do.

Making the Most of Consumer Statements

You have the right to disclose the reasons for a period of delinquencies. For example, if you are laid off for five months and are aware your payments are becoming late, you can place a statement explaining your period of unemployment. If your report shows all good marks before that period and a quick recovery after that period, that explanation will be very valuable to future creditors in evaluating your creditworthiness.

If you dispute an item but aren't successful in getting it removed, you can place a statement explaining your evidence that it is in error. It isn't the outcome that you want, but it is a step in the right direction.

Splitting Accounts in a Divorce

If a former spouse is required by your divorce to pay an account that's in your name, you can have your credit report indicate this arrangement. It might or might not make much difference to future creditors since you are ultimately still legally liable for the debt. But it might help you explain an otherwise clean report, especially if the account has fallen behind.

The best advice is don't let this happen. You can avoid such situations by having the divorce settlement require payments on any debts in your name come directly to you so you can control the manner of payments to your creditor.

Following Up with the Credit Bureau

If you've requested changes or additions, don't assume they'll be made. Establish a reminder system for yourself to make sure everything gets fixed. If you've asked the credit bureaus to make changes to your reports, they should send you amended reports; if you don't receive them within six weeks, follow up. This brings up another reason to check your reports regularly: sometimes the changes don't stick and you need to fix them again. Never assume a change you've seen once is permanent.

The Least You Need to Know

- You have the right to have erroneous information removed from your credit report.

- Sometimes errors originate at the creditor rather than at the credit bureau; in these cases, the credit bureau can't help you fix them.

- If you try to eliminate derogatory marks by challenging accurate information, you might or might not be successful.

- You can place consumer statements on your reports explaining your side of a disputed item or a period of late payments.

Developing a Good Credit Report After Problems

In This Chapter

- Items that lead to a good credit report
- Items that can damage a credit report
- Ways your financial behavior is reflected on your credit report
- Shortcuts to rebuilding a good report

A favorite saying of financial planners is that you can't deduct your way to riches. Said differently, if you make investment decisions based on only whether the investment is tax-deductible, you will miss some beneficial opportunities.

A similar maxim holds true for your credit report. If you live your life to create a perfect credit report, you'll miss some rewarding opportunities. Instead, live your life to meet your needs and maximize your opportunities, and a good credit report will follow.

What Looks Good

When people think of their credit record, they usually are drawn to their payment histories: have they consistently made on-time payments? But so much more goes into the decision to extend credit to a potential borrower. Let's go through some of the important things lenders look at.

Employment

Your employment history is probably the best example of this advice. It's true that working at the same company for 15 years looks better on your credit report than working for 15 employers for a year each. But what if that trek through various employers allowed you to earn three times what you would have earned if you had stayed at the first one? I'll bet your credit report will reflect a higher net worth, a better payment history with your creditors, and lower outstanding debt.

Make your employment decisions based on a long-term view to your employability and financial security. Changing employers frequently might imply instability to a potential creditor, but if the change was to increase your income or further other career goals, it won't get in your way in the long run.

To Your Credit _____

As you come out of a time of financial
stress, your best friend will be cash.
You can use it to secure credit cards,
put higher down payments on cars and
homes, build an emergency fund, and
keep your current obligations current. Don't
let your guard down and think that you
can spend money at a higher level. Use
your cash to stabilize your credit picture
and financial security.

Residence

How frequently you change your residence is also
a stability factor that potential creditors consider.
They will wonder whether they'll be able to find
you if you stop paying your bills. But as with
employment, if you are moving because of family
issues, such as new children or a divorce, it won't be
hard to explain.

Make moving decisions first to satisfy your needs
and life goals. If you are rebuilding a credit report
and can stabilize your address, however, it certainly
can't hurt.

Closed Accounts

Closing accounts you aren't using can help bring
down your outstanding credit. This will be beneficial in overall *credit capacity*.

def•i•ni•tion

Credit capacity is the amount of credit that a creditor determines a consumer can handle, given income and other obligations.

But it will not be helpful in two other calculations that impact your credit score. If the account still has a balance to be paid off and some recent late pays, it's more beneficial to keep it open because most revolving accounts report fewer than seven years of activity. Let's say a department store card reports 36 months of activity. Your late pay last month will automatically disappear from your report in 36 months if you are still making payments. If you pay off and close the account today, that negative information will remain for the full seven years.

The other impact the account will have is to improve your ratio of available credit to outstanding balances. Advice directly from Fair Isaacs seems to contradict itself on this issue. They advise not to use all the credit you have been granted and, at the same time, only apply for credit you'll need. The only way to reconcile these two notions is to have accounts where you have only used a portion of the available credit, but don't have accounts you've never used.

Active Consumer of Credit Services

Have you noticed how smart those coupon machines are at the checkout counters? If you buy Gatorade, you get a coupon for Powerade to use the next time you are in the store. Credit reports are probably the first example of this type of cross-selling. If you are a good customer with Chase, Washington Mutual sends you offers in the mail. And being a good consumer of credit services doesn't just mean you pay your bill on time. It means you actually use credit, go into debt, and pay interest to someone. This is probably the best example of how not to live your life to create a good credit report. You'll be just fine if you never pay a penny of interest on an unsecured debt.

To Your Credit

If you have the opportunity to work with existing creditors to keep one or more accounts open and active, they will become the basis of a new good report. The accounts that have been opened the longest will hold the most weight in most credit analyses.

Mortgage Histories

Probably the most important thing on your credit report is your mortgage payment history. Creditors know your home is very important to you and that you will probably make that payment before everything else. If you let it go late, that speaks volumes to your next creditor. Credit reports reflect payments as late only if they are paid 30 days or more after the due date.

Many people pay in the grace period between the 1st and 15th of each month. Even though this is not reflected on the credit report, your mortgage company does report this directly when a new mortgage company asks for a payment history. You can be labeled a "slow payer" even though your credit report is perfect.

What Can Hurt

You already know different creditors consider different criteria as negative. Some items that can appear negative have more to do with your behavior as a consumer of credit services than they do with whether you pay your bills on time. For instance, if you are a 50-year-old with two positive items both relating to home mortgages on your report and nothing else—no credit card accounts or auto financing—you will raise suspicion that you must have declared bankruptcy 11 years ago. It's not believable that you just didn't like debt and never opened any accounts.

Finance Companies

Finance companies are firms that charge high interest rates for loans usually collateralized by consumer items. One finance company will not look at another finance company reference on your report as negative, but banks and mortgage companies might look at a history of using finance company loans as evidence that maybe your credit hasn't always been stellar or that you are not the best decision maker. Why would you pay 25 percent interest for money if you have good credit? So the presence of finance company loans on your report can be considered derogatory.

Churning Credit Cards

Remember the days of 18 percent credit card rates? That rate was so universal it almost seemed like price fixing in a day of 7 percent mortgages and 9 percent car loans. Eventually, market pressure took over, and good-credit households started receiving baskets of offers to complete *balance transfers* to new accounts with lower rates. Many of these have unbelievably low teaser rates for six months. People churn their balances by moving from one card to another as these teaser rates expire. It's a time-consuming, but profitable, game.

def•i•ni•tion

A **balance transfer** is the movement of funds from one debt account to another, commonly used with credit card balances to achieve a lower-interest rate.

Even though the credit card companies set themselves up for this behavior among consumers, they like to complain about customers who do it, calling them credit jumpers, and might shy away from you if they don't think they'll keep you for long.

Inquiry Activity

If you were shopping for a car, to shop around and look for the best deal would be a very responsible consumer behavior. But if you are financing the car, the dealer wouldn't know the best deal for you until he pulled your credit report because the dealer doesn't just sell the car—he sells the money that goes with it. So in one day, you could rack up six or seven credit inquiries—without even purchasing one car yet.

The credit-scoring system dings you for excessive inquiries because creditors don't like people who shop around for credit. They're also concerned that recent inquiries could mean you have other credit applications pending and could have more outstanding than you've disclosed. The FACT Act of 2003 (see Chapter 12) changed how credit scores can weigh these reasonable requests for your report that relate to activities such as car shopping.

The Behavior Behind the Report

No credit-reporting system can ever tell potential creditors, employers, and insurance companies exactly what kind of credit consumer you will be. Instead, the credit-reporting system provides creditors and others interested in your credit history with data they can compare with the history they have had with their customer base over the years. For instance, a creditor might have learned that people who have declared bankruptcy are 10 times more likely to embezzle than those who haven't, so a bankruptcy in your past could take you out of the running for a job managing the company's bank accounts. Does this mean you are an embezzler? Not at all, but the company has found an easy way to minimize its risk of hiring embezzlers.

Creditors, employers, and even insurance companies have strict rules about whom they can discriminate against. So far, people with bad credit are not a protected class, by themselves. The rules are difficult, though, so if by using a certain credit criteria a mortgage company ends up leaving out an entire neighborhood which happens to house only senior citizens, they could be accused of inadvertently discriminating on the basis of age.

A Good Customer or Trustworthy Employee

Put yourself in your creditor's position for a second. Whom would you want as a customer? Now pretend you're an employer. What kind of financial position would make you trust a potential employee? Each creditor and employer would give answers to satisfy their own particular needs. How much they have at risk, how badly they need more customers or employees, and what their competition is up to would all come into play.

A Profitable Customer or Productive Employee

Many sales managers know that salespeople who have a lot of personal debt are more motivated to close deals quickly so they can make the next car payment or house payment. They don't want someone who reneges on their responsibilities, though, so they might be more interested in someone with a high debt-to-income ratio and a history of on-time payments.

A finance company might be more interested in someone with low debt. Because they charge such high interest rates, they can afford to accept folks with a few dings in their payment histories, as long as it looks like they can afford the payment now.

Tips to Get It Going Quickly

The biggest mistake people with damaged credit make is to think they've just been locked up for seven years and can't do anything about it. This is the furthest thing from the truth. In fact, if they do nothing for seven years, they won't have a good report then, either. They'll have *no* report. However, if they immediately start building good references, in seven years they'll have seven-year-old strong references.

To Your Credit

Consumer Action, at www.consumer-action.org, is a nonprofit consumer advisory organization that offers lists of secured cards and low-rate cards. It also provides dozens of helpful online informational articles on every aspect of personal financial management.

Secured Credit

Find the lowest-limit, lowest-fee *secured credit card* offered today. Appendix B has several references to get you started. Make a deposit to a savings account, and the bank will issue you a Visa or MasterCard with that same limit. You don't have to use it, but as you deposit more into the savings account, your limit will raise. If you do use it and make payments on time, you can ask for a limit raise that doesn't have to be secured. At some point in the future, you can ask for the collateral to be released altogether.

def•i•ni•tion

A **secured credit card** is a credit card that is backed by a savings account equal to or greater than the credit limit on the card.

When your bad marks are eliminated, you'll have a long-term good credit reference. Having a secured card is often enough to qualify you for instant credit at department stores, and you'll be able to build your credit very quickly. But do not apply for cards before you are fairly sure you will qualify. Applying for credit and being turned down adds inquiries that don't have corresponding credit references—something you want to avoid because it looks suspicious.

Another way to build credit references is, instead of using cash to purchase an appliance or vehicle, to use that cash as collateral for a bank or credit union loan, which you then can use to buy the appliance or vehicle. The cash in the bank might actually allow you to get a very low interest rate, while at the same time helping you build your report. Keep in mind, however, that these loans need to be longer than six months to really do you any good.

Credit Cautions

When shopping for a secured credit card, don't forget you are still the customer and have a lot of options. Many of these companies prey on the fact that you feel like a second-class citizen and have nowhere else to turn for a card. Use one of the many websites in Appendix B to compare offers.

Co-Signed Credit and Authorized User Accounts

Another form of security for your creditors is to have creditworthy people sign loans with you or add you as an *authorized user* on their accounts. I usually advise against people doing this for you because it places their report at risk if you fall behind on your portion of the payment. But if they love you and are ready to pay the payments if you don't, it can help you get back on your feet quickly. Loans in your name, co-signed by others, will likely be reported on your credit report, but credit cards where you are only an authorized user will not enhance your credit score under the latest formulas.

def•i•ni•tion

An **authorized user** is anyone who is legally allowed to incur debt on a credit card in your name. You are liable for all charges incurred by their use of the account.

Adding Nonreporting Creditors to Your Report

As noted in Chapter 7, chances are good you have financial obligations that have not made it to your credit report. Landlords are a good example of this type of creditor because most don't take the time to report to the national agencies. Many use local companies that specialize in rental histories. If your credit history with them is good, you can request their history be added to your credit reports.

Other creditors, such as family members, don't hold much weight with major creditors, but building a report after a period of negative information is a process, and these references certainly won't hurt. (See Chapter 13 for a sample letter requesting a history with a nonreporting creditor be added to your report.)

Unlike some challenges in life, bad credit is something you can definitely recover from. It's also something you can continue to damage if you don't pay attention to how it got that way in the first place. Change your personal financial behavior today to ensure a wonderful credit report in the future.

The Least You Need to Know

- Make good decisions first, and watch your credit report reflect them.

- Use the seven years that your report will hold negative information to build a very strong positive report.

- Secured credit cards are the fastest and easiest way to begin to recover from a bad credit report.

- You can request that creditors not currently reporting to the credit-reporting agencies be added.

Chapter 9

Preventing Identity Theft

In This Chapter

- The difference between fraud and identity theft
- Finding out whether you have been victimized
- Protecting yourself from identity theft
- Where to get help

Old-fashioned con artists had to be clever to impersonate you. They might have mastered your signature or disguised themselves to look like you, but they had to be fast talkers and quick thinkers. Unfortunately, times have changed. A few carefully typed account numbers, and they are you!

Fraud has been around for centuries. What we now refer to as identity theft is a type of fraud made possible by the information age. As you work to develop a perfect credit report, you become more attractive as a mark for these criminals. But you can use different strategies to protect yourself, so let's learn about them.

What You Can Do

Identity thieves don't have to be too clever in these complicated times. Information is everywhere, and with a little bit of deliberate thievery, they have the benefit of all the years of hard work you've spent to build your creditworthiness. They can find your personal information through a variety of tried-and-true techniques, including the following:

- Stealing your mail
- Submitting a change of address for you at the post office or with your credit card companies
- Going through trash at businesses where you shop
- Stealing files from companies where you have accounts
- Tricking you into giving them your information over the phone or online
- Stealing your purse or wallet
- Posing as a potential landlord or employer to order your credit report
- Breaking into your home and stealing your records
- Hacking into electronic files at your bank or credit card company

With this information, they can get into just about any trouble you could get into on your own, except they don't have to suffer the consequences. You do.

They could …

- Commit any number of crimes and identify themselves as you.
- Open new checking and credit accounts in your name, using them but never making deposits or payments.
- Rent apartments and never pay the rent.
- Rent cars to steal them.
- Buy or lease cars in your name, never making the payments.
- Establish utility, cable, or cellular service in your name.

Some of these actions can result in criminal trouble, some in financial trouble, and others in credit report dings. To be confronted with this type of trauma when you've done nothing wrong is the ultimate frustration. In fact, you've done everything right: you've created a reputation that allows the thief to enjoy the amount of credit that makes you a good target for this crime.

Fraud has always been a crime. Entering into transactions under false pretenses with the intention of harming someone else can involve numerous forms of lying and deceit. The crime of fraud turns the corner into identity theft when the criminal pretends to be you and harms you in the process. Chances are, someone who steals your identity will be charged with fraud, if caught. The crime of identity theft is rarely prosecuted because the underlying fraud is much easier to prove.

Know Your Information

As a financial advisor, I met people daily who didn't know where they kept certain information that was essential to helping them develop a good financial strategy. It was great when someone actually showed up with all these papers together, with everything in order and easy to work with.

Having all your current account numbers easily accessible makes it easier to cross-check your credit reports when you review them. When you order your yearly reports, make sure all the accounts on the report are actually yours. Unless you cross-check account numbers, you might not notice a stray account with a creditor you do business with.

> **Credit Cautions** _____
>
> Don't forget that even family members can steal your identity and open accounts in your name. In fact, people who end up committing this crime for a living likely practiced on their family first. Keep all statements, account numbers, and passwords locked away so as not to tempt anyone.

Because some of the accounts a thief might open in your name won't show up on your credit report until they are sent to a collection agency, a clean credit report is not conclusive evidence that your identity isn't being used without your consent. Once a cellular phone bill is run up and not paid, for example, it takes several months to go to a collection agency and be reflected on your credit report. Having good records is the first step in what might be a long path to proving that you had nothing to do with that bill.

Protect Your Numbers

These documents, however, pose some increased risk in a world with identity thieves. Some people find it helpful to keep computer files listing all their accounts and numbers. The best strategy is to keep them on a thumb drive that is password-protected, not on your hard drive, which might be open to hacking through your Internet connections.

Lock files of account numbers you keep at home so that, at a minimum, a home invader would be delayed in getting to them. And get a personal shredder to make it next to impossible to piece back together key information you send to the city dump.

To Your Credit

The Identity Theft Resource Center, at www.idtheftcenter.org, is a nationwide nonprofit organization dedicated to helping victims and informing consumers of prevention strategies.

The most powerful number to a thief is your Social Security number, and many people now understand that. Some states allow individuals to remove their

Social Security number from their driver's license. This way they're not carrying it around wherever they go, and if they lose their wallet, it isn't out there for the picking. Never give it out except in legitimate circumstances for legitimate purposes.

Keep Only Accounts That You Monitor

You're at the Sears Hardware checkout line, and the clerk asks if you want to save $10 on your purchases today by opening an account. You think, okay, sure. Why not?

A couple weeks later, the card is mailed to you, but you never receive it because someone steals it from your mail. You don't even remember you opened the account. You got your $10 discount, and you're happy. This card now purchases several power tools, which can be easily hocked for cash. Then the thief ditches the card, but not before he uses the name and address to learn more about you and uses that information to open other accounts.

At the same time, he changes the address and phone number on the accounts so you never see the bills or hear from the collectors. A few months later, you get a notice from another Visa account that you still use that your account has been cancelled due to derogatory information on your credit report. It must be a mistake. But it's not. They have based their decision on an account that was used fraudulently, but it was still your account—and you will be guilty until you prove yourself innocent.

Open only accounts you need and intend to use regularly so you will notice if the bill doesn't come or if the balance is inexplicably high.

Credit Cautions

As difficult as identity theft is to deal with because it happens without your knowledge, most consumer fraud in this country actually has willing victims. People are duped every day by crooks selling them scams or getting their account numbers with their permission. Be very vigilant with your good name.

Look At Your Reports Regularly

As much as we might complain about the credit bureaus' inefficiencies and mistakes, in this area they provide us a great service. It's very difficult for an identity thief to keep his or her activities off your credit reports. Since you have access to your reports whenever you want, that should be a deterrent. The problem is that most people don't look at their reports except when they apply for credit—and not even then, in many cases.

The three major bureaus all have monitoring services that alert you when you request your report. If you subscribe to this service and someone uses your name to apply for credit, you'll be alerted that something illegal might be happening even before the account can be opened and certainly before it can be used. By subscribing to these services, you can let the credit bureaus tell you when there is activity in your name, which shortens the time between when an identity thief begins his attack on your credit and when you learn about it.

To Your Credit

The Privacy Rights Clearinghouse, at www.privacyrights.org, has facts sheets available on a range of privacy topics. It also provides support services for identity theft victims.

If something looks fishy, don't apologize for asking the credit bureau for an explanation. You'll be the one explaining it for a long time to come if it's an illegal activity. Make sure that you understand every line on your report, even if it looks positive. People sometimes make the mistake of challenging an item on their report and being satisfied when it is removed, not realizing it is an early warning signal of identity theft.

How to Recover If It Happens to You

The longer the thief is active, the more damage he or she can do, and the longer it will take you to unravel it all. You should take several basic steps initially and then more steps as you begin to determine how extensive the damage was:

1. Notify the banks and creditors directly involved to close accounts and issue you new account numbers. Your liability for credit accounts is limited to $50 unless you have a *zero liability* account. It's likely you'll have less protection for debit cards and checking account thefts, depending upon your institution. Usually, you can get your money back when you show your signature was forged.

def•i•ni•tion

The **zero liability** feature on credit card accounts means that your credit card issuer assumes all liability for unauthorized purchases on your card. There might be restrictions on this feature, but it can be helpful if your account numbers have been stolen.

2. File a police report, listing all the involved accounts. You'll need this report when you begin the process of restoring your credit.

3. Place an initial fraud security alert on all three credit reports. Each bureau has a special division dedicated to receiving this information and helping consumers understand how to manage their credit report through this crisis. Contact one of the credit-reporting agencies at the following numbers to report identity theft. The agency you contact will forward your alert to the other two.

TransUnion Fraud Alert
PO Box 6790
Fullerton, CA 92834
www.transunion.com
1-800-680-7289
714-447-6034 fax

Equifax Consumer Fraud Division
PO Box 740256
Atlanta, GA 30374
www.equifax.com
1-800-525-6285
770-375-2821 fax

Experian's National Consumer Assistance
PO Box 9530
Allen, TX 75013
www.experian.com
1-888-397-3742

4. The last report you should file is with the Federal Trade Commission's Consumer Response Center. It collects reports and offers tremendous resources for where to turn next. It has developed an ID Theft Affidavit that is becoming widely accepted as a tool for creditors and others to verify what has happened to you. Its contact information is:

Federal Trade Commission
600 Pennsylvania Ave., N.W.
Washington, DC 20580
www.ftc.gov/idtheft
1-877-IDTHEFT (1-877-438-4338)

Depending upon your specific situation, you might need to take several more actions.

The Least You Need to Know

- Keep your records updated and safe from home invaders and computer hackers.

- Protect your Social Security number and other account numbers by using them only when you initiate the transaction. Carry with you only cards you need.

- Your credit reports are your best early-detection device for identity theft; order them regularly or use the credit bureau's alert services.

- If you are a victim of identity theft, you'll spend a lot of time defending your good name. Be very systematic, and keep good records of your defense.

Chapter 10

The Credit-Repair Industry

In This Chapter

- What credit-repair companies can do
- What credit-repair companies can't do
- The regulation of the credit-repair industry
- How to spot scams

Credit-repair companies came onto the scene with a bang in the mid-eighties. Many were initially structured as multi-level marketing companies (like Amway or Mary Kay) and held meetings every night of the week to inform consumers of the evils of the credit-reporting industry. It didn't take long before they attracted attention from regulators, not to mention the credit bureaus. Today, credit-repair companies are much more discreet, following new laws that curtail their activities. As you investigate this option for your situation, learn as much as you can about the company you are dealing with. This information can help you decide whether to use their services.

What They Do

At their most basic, credit-repair companies are efficient secretarial services. At their most advanced, they are legal-advice companies guiding you through every loophole in the law they can find. They base most of their activity on the Fair Credit Reporting Act provision that requires credit bureaus to verify within 30 days any item you challenge as inaccurate on your report. After 30 days of *nonverification*, the law requires the reference be removed from your report until it is verified.

def•i•ni•tion

The **nonverification** of an account occurs 30 days after a credit bureau is asked to verify a debt at the consumer's request. If the bureau cannot confirm the accuracy of the item, under law, the information must be removed from the file until verified.

Credit-repair companies take advantage of this provision by inundating all the credit bureaus with dozens of letters requesting verification of any aspect of a negative credit reference. The assumption is that some will not make the 30-day deadline.

Promises Made

A Google search on the Internet returns more than a million hits with the term *credit repair*, which should tell you right away that a lot of companies are out there trying to profit from your bad credit. Reading through the teaser ads would have you believe that there is a guaranteed way to clean up your report.

Promises Kept

The promises vary from firm to firm. Read carefully to see if you are buying a time period during which they will service your report, a number of challenges to correct or remove information, or some other measurement of service. Read even more carefully to find out just what they are guaranteeing. Some firms promise to send out letters and charge for only the items they succeed in getting removed from your report.

Most of the firms will go through the motions that they promise. They will challenge all items that are not in *good standing*. What they can't control is how the credit bureau will respond. Some of the items they ask to be verified will be verified. Then what? Do it again, until they cry, "Uncle!"?

def•i•ni•tion

> An account is in **good standing** when it is currently paid as agreed.

Is it really worth it to pay a company to try to repair your credit? For some people, in some situations, it can be.

Their Value to You

If you are eager to begin the process of getting your report under control because you know inaccurate items are on it, but you really have no time to generate letters and follow up, these firms might provide a valuable service.

However, if you buy into their promises that they can somehow control the behavior of the credit bureaus and your creditors, then their value is hard to measure. Let's say you have six dings on your reports. A credit-repair company goes to work and eliminates four. That's a very respectable result, actually. But still two remain. How much does that really help? These two dings are probably still enough to keep you from qualifying for the best interest rates.

What They Can't Do

To put it bluntly, credit-repair companies can't break the law. Even though several laws allow them to request investigations of your inaccurate items, they can't challenge every little item just because it looks bad. This practice has been addressed by legislation, allowing the credit bureaus to ignore fallacious requests.

They also can't help you commit fraud by starting a new credit report using a new Social Security number or other identity. It would be nice to be able to just start over again, but short of being in the witness-protection program, it's unlikely to happen legally. Having your debts *discharged* by bankruptcy is kind of like a new start, but the credit report reference remains visible for at least seven years. It's a little like getting all dressed up to impress a new date and then getting sprayed with mud before you reach the curb. (For more on bankruptcy, see Chapter 11.)

def•i•ni•tion

A debtor is **discharged** or released from the obligation of repaying a debt when a bankruptcy is completed.

They Can't Change Your Behavior

Ten years ago, when the legislators in my state tried to outlaw credit-repair practices, they gave up and regulated them instead. They required that firms be licensed and bonded and that fees be paid only after the service was rendered. As the state agency charged with enforcing the regulations went looking for credit-repair companies, it cast a rather wide net and found me, a financial counselor. I laughed because the last thing I wanted was to give my clients a quick fix.

You see, I had been working for years with people whose credit was damaged, and I have to admit I appreciated the fact that my clients couldn't run out and jump into more debt right away. That gave me time to work through the behavioral issues that had started the whole mess. As the behaviors improved, the credit report improved, and life became work-able again. My clients had new approaches to man-aging their money and a new appreciation for the power of their creditworthiness.

Every alcoholic knows that a drink will fix his hang-over. Most people in debt believe another loan will fix the problems left over from the last one. They're all wrong. The hair of the dog only gives the illu-sion that the problem has gone away. It will be back, and it will bite harder.

Credit Cautions

Never make a decision that will impact your credit report negatively with the intention of cleaning it up later. Make every effort to find ways to manage your money well and work with your creditors.

If you have addressed, honestly and completely, the behavioral chains that have been holding you down, then you deserve good credit. You can and should do everything in your power to develop a credit report that reflects your new approach to managing your money. But if you believe all your problems will be solved permanently just by fixing your credit report, you're mistaken. It will be a Band-Aid on a cancer. It will look better on the surface, but under-neath, the problem will still be festering.

If you clear your credit report before you have adopted new financial-management strategies, you will possibly be doing yourself more harm than good. Access to credit is the last thing you need if you are still prone to overusing it.

They Can't Change Your Ex-Spouse's Behavior

When a couple divorces, both people make a list of all their debts and divide them up using some agreed-upon criteria. Many times, the assets that go with those debts determine who gets the debt. He gets the motorcycle payment; she gets the house payment; he gets the Firestone charge; and she gets the Victoria's Secret account. Problems arise when he was the one who opened the Victoria's Secret account and she's now the one responsible for paying it back. If she decides she's not going to pay off the balance, it's not her credit that's going to be affected: it's his.

Credit-repair companies might be successful in removing dings caused by such a situation, but they won't be able to prevent your ex from adding more dings to your account. The only way to avoid dings is to make the payments yourself on accounts that have your name on them. If your ex should be paying it, he or she could pay you directly as a property settlement. But most divorce settlements don't get this clever.

They Can't Change Your Creditor's Behavior

Your creditors handle millions of pieces of information every minute. Your credit report is a tadpole swimming in an ocean of data. If you clean it up through requests for verification and something accurate is removed because it can't be verified, it can still reappear. Your creditors usually send data to the bureaus every month. They know you were late three times in 2008, so your credit reference from them reflects that. When you ask for an unverifiable item to be removed, the credit bureau will remove it. However, when the creditor reports on you next month, it might still have a record of your three late payments, causing the information to reappear. It's always a gamble to try to remove negative yet accurate information because it might show up again anytime.

How to Spot Credit-Repair Scams

Desperate people sometimes overlook common warning signs in the marketplace. When you have bad credit—and all the insecure feelings that come with that—you aren't likely to ask really tough questions of someone who promises to get you out of that situation. But in credit repair, as in the rest of the world, if it sounds too good to be true, it probably is. If you know that everything bad on your report is totally untrue, these firms might be able to help you. If you are hoping they can remove accurate information, be prepared to see them fail.

State Regulators and Licensing Agencies

Each state handles the credit-repair industry a little differently. To find a list of licensed credit-repair companies in your state, you can start with your Department of Commerce or your attorney general's office. If your state licenses credit-repair companies, there is, no doubt, a system for complaints. Find out whether the complaints are available to the public; if they are, such information can give you some insight into the company you're considering working with.

Be very wary of doing business with someone outside your state unless you are fully prepared to have no recourse if the company scams you. Fighting with a local company is hard enough. Fighting with a company across the state line can be downright discouraging. Don't ask for more headaches than you already have.

Better Business Bureaus and Other Watchdogs

Consumer watchdogs and mediation services can usually provide you with ratings or histories of fair business practices of firms you are considering working with. Before you sign up for a service, take a minute to call the Better Business Bureau (BBB) in the area where the company is located. You might find that a company promises your money back if you are not satisfied, but that several consumers had trouble getting the business to make good on that promise.

Credit Cautions

Before you sign any contract with a credit-repair firm, check with the Better Business Bureau (BBB) in the area where the credit-repair company does business to see if there have been complaints. You can find local BBB branches online at www.bbb.org.

The Least You Need to Know

- The credit-repair industry has been highly scrutinized and regulated because of a less-than-reputable past.

- You should develop your own strategy for managing your credit report and delegate only those tasks that make sense to you.

- Check out thoroughly any firm you are considering doing business with.

- Repairing your credit without readjusting your behavior is futile.

Where to Find Help

In This Chapter

- How credit-counseling agencies work
- What bankruptcy attorneys can do for you
- Other actions you might need an attorney to help with
- The role of financial counseling in credit problems

When you need help evaluating your credit report problems, you might not have the necessary money to pay for competent advice. Relying on free sources presents a dilemma: Why is it free, and who is paying for it? Relying on attorneys usually steers you to a bankruptcy conversation, which you may or may not need. Here is some insight to help you determine who might have the best advice for you. (Don't forget to check out Appendix B for additional resources that might help.)

Credit-Counseling Agencies

Credit-counseling agencies have a deservedly varied reputation in the United States. This segment of the credit and collection industry was started a half-century ago by department stores that wanted to collect the consumer debt owed to them and, at the same time, maintain a good reputation with their customer base. Instead of having their employees call delinquent customers to collect their "charge card" balances, they funded separate agencies to hang out signs advertising to help folks in trouble with their bills. When those folks walked into the counseling agencies willingly, the department stores found it was much more likely to work out a plan that was fair to all the creditors. When the person behind on payments regained financial footing, she would be back at the department store as a good customer, without the sting of having dealt with collectors directly associated with the store.

As the agencies expanded their role as benevolent collectors, they encouraged other creditors to accept negotiated payments from them. They kept a portion of the amounts collected, sometimes referring to it as the fair share. This amount, usually 15 percent, looked amazingly similar to the commission charged by third-party collection agencies for performing a similar task. The difference was that this collection agency (a.k.a. credit-counseling agency) was initiating the transaction. The creditor had not asked the agency to collect the debt. Nonetheless, most creditors were happy enough to pay for the services, as long as it meant that debtors were paying their debts and avoiding filing for bankruptcy.

Credit Cautions

Nothing is free. Understand who is paying for a service before you use it. If it is you, understand all the fees before you start. If it is someone else, find out why they are doing it.

By the late 1990s agencies were advertising nationwide and providing services over the phone and the Internet. At the same time, the success rates of most firms dropped to all-time lows. Fewer than 10 percent of consumers actually stayed with programs long enough to repay all their debts, and the creditors began imposing quality guidelines on the companies. They also lowered the amount they were willing to have withheld as the agency's fair share, putting pressure on the firms to be more efficient. Today there are hundreds of firms to choose from across the country, with a couple dozen industry leaders doing business nationwide.

There is an artificial debate about whether it is better to do business with a firm that is for-profit or nonprofit. For the most part, the nonprofit firms are wholly funded by the creditors or are front organizations for for-profit companies. The for-profits are accused of charging unfair fees and have been regulated out of business in many states.

Congress is looking into the question of whether these nonprofit companies fall under one of the legitimate tax-exempt categories, and we might see some changes in the coming years.

Although the services that such firms offer vary greatly, I'll walk you through the basic ways they can help.

Budgeting Help

Most credit-counseling firms provide what they call "budgeting help." When you sign up, you fill out a standard budget form, which they evaluate to see if you have enough disposable income to pay the minimum they feel they'll need to negotiate with your creditors usually 2 percent of your outstanding balances. So if you owe $10,000 and your budget shows an extra $200 per month, they'll accept you into their program. If you don't show an extra $200, they'll probe further. Can you earn more money? Cut more expenses? In essence, how can you fit into their program?

Whether such services count as budgeting help is debatable. Certainly, the mere activity of thinking through and writing down all your expenses is a great start to getting control of your debt and your credit report. But the amount of actual time they spend with you and how much follow-up they do as credit counselors is usually very limited. If you expect to receive credit counseling, ask up front how much time, on average, they spend with clients and what training their counselors have in the area.

They'll usually limit their interaction with you to discussion of the accounts they're paying on your behalf. The rest of your budget is yours to manage on your own.

Debt-Repayment Plans

The process of collecting a lump sum from consumers and distributing it equally among their creditors is called *pro-rating* (and the firms that specialize in this practice are called pro-raters). With pressure from the larger creditors, the credit-counseling companies often send preferred creditors more than their pro-rated share of your money, leaving smaller creditors, such as doctors, waiting for their money or getting much smaller relative payments.

def•i•ni•tion

> **Pro-rating** is the process of repaying your debts in a proportionate fashion, usually by sending your disposable income to a third party, such as a bankruptcy trustee or a credit-counseling program. For example, if a creditor represents 25 percent of your outstanding debt, it would receive 25 percent of the money you apply to all your debts.

You can benefit from the preferential treatment credit-counseling agencies give to the larger creditors. For instance, the preferential treatment gives the credit-counseling agencies bargaining power to negotiate lower interest rates for your accounts and get late fees reduced or waived. However, if you don't finish the repayment program, the credit card companies can go back and recalculate the interest and late fees you would have been charged.

Because of the very poor performance of these firms in recent years, creditors began offering these same plans directly to their debtors. So before you sign up for a credit-counseling plan, call your creditors and ask them what plans they can offer you. You may find that included in what they can do for you is a process called re-aging, where after making a set amount of payments on time, all past due amounts are erased. This will leave your credit report in much better condition than if you had used a credit-counseling program.

Do They Help or Hurt Your Report?

When you engage the services of a credit-counseling firm, the business normally places a reference on your credit reports indicating it is working for you. Many creditors find this a derogatory mark, with the logic being that only people looking for a way to get out of paying the previously contracted amounts on their credit accounts would use such a firm. Because it is viewed as negative, it falls under the same guidelines as other dings and must remain for seven years.

To Your Credit

Many creditors now have internal recovery programs where they work directly with their customers to help them pay off their accounts. For instance, they offer re-aging programs that report an account paid on time after a customer makes three or six on-time payments. Ask your creditors whether they have such programs before you sign up for a credit-counseling program. You might find you can impact your credit report much more positively through their internal recovery programs.

The credit-counseling industry would disagree, arguing that working with these firms shows a willingness to repay all your debts, even in hard times. The firms will boast they have many successful customers who can finance homes and cars after finishing their program. Although it's certainly true that these auto loans and home mortgages are available to people with bad credit references, the interest rate is usually much higher.

If your report is already dinged up due to late payments on several accounts, a reference indicating you are working with a credit-counseling firm probably isn't going to do that much more damage—especially if by working with them you find a way to get out of debt faster.

So here's the short answer: if your report is fine and you want to open a credit-counseling account only to get your interest rates lowered, don't do it. You'll damage your report by doing so.

Bankruptcy Attorneys

Bankruptcy petitions must be filed in a special federal court. Because bankruptcy is a unique area of law, attorneys tend to specialize in that area. It is possible to represent yourself in bankruptcy court, and more people are trying to do so to save the fees. However, since the 2005 revisions to the bankruptcy laws, representing yourself is much more complicated, and one small mistake can get your case dismissed.

One of the changes since 2005 is that bankruptcy filers must complete pre-filing and pre-discharge education. This normally takes the place of a computerized curriculum but can be classes at the bankruptcy trustee's office or other agencies. This has been a big step forward in recognizing that the legal remedies are only one part of turning around an individual's financial life. But the trainings are short and don't usually offer one-on-one counseling.

Two chapters of the bankruptcy code routinely apply to individuals: Chapter 7 and Chapter 13.

To Your Credit

By definition, most bankruptcy attorneys' clients are bankrupt, meaning they owe more than they own. How, you must be wondering, do they make a living working for people with more debts than money? The answer is simple: they get their money up front by telling their clients to immediately stop paying all other creditors. As soon as they get enough money for their fee, they go to work, or they are paid through the repayment plan administered by the bankruptcy trustee.

Chapter 7 Filings

Chapter 7 allows a debtor to liquidate all nonexempt assets and pay the proceeds toward all debts, while being released from all obligations on any balance left.

When a debtor files for bankruptcy, his creditors are invited to file their *claims* stating what they believe he owes them. The action *stays* any collection activity from creditors and provides immediate protection from garnishment, seizure of assets, and collection phone calls and letters. Chapter 7 filings may remain on your credit report for 10 years. However, for loans over $50,000, these time limits do not apply, so theoretically at least, the record can remain forever. Also, many insurance, employment, and credit applications ask directly if you have ever filed a Chapter 7, so even if your credit report doesn't list the filing, the action will follow you forever.

def•i•ni•tion

A **claim** is a filing by a creditor in a bankruptcy case stating that the debtor owes him money. A **stay** is a stopping action by the bankruptcy judge to stop all creditor action toward the debtor, including mail, phone calls, and any garnishments.

Chapter 13 Filings

Chapter 13 filings also immediately stop all collection actions from the creditors. People with more assets than liabilities often use this option, usually to save a home or car from being seized by the creditor. Instead of liquidating assets to repay a portion of the debt, the debtor pledges a portion of his future earnings to repay a portion or all of the outstanding debt. This is sometimes called a wage earner's plan. Repayment plans proposed to the court, which sets the repayment section and amount of repayment, can go as low as 5 percent of the outstanding balances and can be scheduled over three to five years, typically.

The Chapter 13 filings remain on the credit report for seven years and are reported to do much less damage to an individual's creditworthiness than Chapter 7 filings. A Chapter 13 plan can also be converted to a Chapter 7 plan if the payments become unaffordable.

Many creditors will consider offering you a standard interest rate one year after you successfully complete a repayment plan. Beware of this segment of the credit industry that looks for customers recently out of bankruptcy, knowing they have few if any obligations left to pay. Their offers may sound attractive, but they can very quickly return you to the overextended condition you just corrected through the bankruptcy.

Credit Cautions

Your attorney is not the best source of information or advice on how a bankruptcy filing affects your credit or how to repair your credit after a bankruptcy. Bankruptcy attorneys rarely have contact with their clients in the years following the bankruptcy filing and don't have experience in managing the negative effects. If you expect your attorney to help you with this, ask him in advance whether he offers this service and if he includes it in his standard fee.

Both types of bankruptcy protection are designed to protect assets and wages from seizure by a single creditor, which would leave all creditors out in the cold.

As an alternative to filing for bankruptcy, some states have voluntary wage-garnishment programs that allow a local court to pro-rate your maximum wage garnishment across all creditors. If you are enrolled in such a program, it will be noted on your credit report and will have the same negative impact that credit counseling and Chapter 13 programs have. They indicate a serious problem with a serious solution, but they also show that the debtor is interested in repaying the debts.

Damage Lawsuits Against Creditors and Bureaus

The federal laws governing the creditors and credit bureaus have become much more strict regarding the protections you enjoy as a consumer (see Chapter 12 for an overview of these laws). The enforcement of these laws, however, is still largely left to the consumer. The Federal Trade Commission and your state attorney general's office might be the most active in prosecuting offenders, but it is still your duty to report violations. When you report violations, don't expect them to represent you personally in any action. Instead, they will collect data until they see a pattern that merits investigation.

To demand compensation for damages done to you, you must bring an action against the creditors and credit bureaus yourself. Taking on huge, attorney-heavy financial institutions isn't a job for every attorney. Some attorneys, albeit very few, specialize in recovering damages caused by creditors and credit-reporting agencies. They usually make their money as a contingent fee based on what they recover for their clients in a lawsuit. There can be a long wait before cases come to trial and money actually changes hands—if it ever does.

The next chapter details most of the laws that protect you. If you feel your rights have been violated and you want to explore the option of a lawsuit, be ready for a long, involved process.

To Your Credit

Occasionally, you might find yourself as a member of a class that is filing a class action lawsuit. When you get notices regarding your claim in the lawsuit, don't ignore them. They could result in interesting settlement offers before they are over.

Financial Counselors

Financial counseling is a relatively new field that combines the knowledge base of financial planners and credit counselors with the strategies of social workers and psychological counselors. For people in debt, financial counselors can help sort out the emotional issues from the financial challenges. Many financial counselors work inside financial institutions such as credit unions. Some are government employees such as Cooperative Extension agents or military counselors. Others work in the social service world through housing agencies, employee-assistance programs, or offices on aging.

Behavioral Help

All financial behaviors are learned, either by watching adults as a child or by trying different approaches as an adult and learning from mistakes. Sometimes financial choices are controlled by other psychological processes, such as alcoholism, which have very little to do with money. When these issues collide, people can benefit from professional counseling from a psychologist or social worker who has some training in financial issues. Many times health insurance partially covers these visits.

Many credit problems stem from compulsive behaviors that are very similar to alcoholism. Compulsive spending, gambling, overeating, and sexual addictions can create severe financial strain and lead to credit abuse and credit problems. Fixing your credit report problems without addressing the underlying issues that led to them will do nothing but send a message to your brain that there is an easy way out of the mess. Fixing the underlying problem is the true solution, but it takes much more commitment and time.

To Your Credit

As soon as you sense any possible trouble with your financial situation, look for guidance. Appendix B has dozens of resources to help you get on the right track.

The Consumer Is King

Unlike credit-counseling agencies, financial and behavioral counselors don't receive any so-called fair share payments from creditors, so there is no conflict of interest. And unlike bankruptcy attorneys, they are not selling a single solution. Instead, financial and behavior counselors can help consumers identify all their options and make decisions in their best interest.

In addition, many financial counselors have been trained to advise people of their rights regarding their credit reports. They work far differently than the credit-repair industry, however. Instead of offering quick fixes, they work with consumers to answer their questions and work out strategies that are in their clients' best interests.

It's never easy to know whom to trust or who will have your interest at heart. You won't often hear your friends bragging about how great their bankruptcy attorney was, so it's hard to know who is good at what he does. If you need to seek advice from someone more knowledgeable, develop a plan for how to find this expert. Use the resources in Appendix B to get started.

The Least You Need to Know

- Credit-counseling agencies can help or hurt your credit report, depending upon your situation.

- Credit-counseling agencies are paid by your creditors and have a very poor track record of actually helping consumers eliminate their debt.

- Bankruptcy attorneys have only two options to propose and are not trained or paid to explore self-managed or credit-counseling options with you.

- Financial counselors can help consumers identify all their options and work out a strategy that best fits their needs.

Chapter 12

The Laws That Are on Your Side

In This Chapter

- Federal laws that govern credit transactions
- Federal laws that protect consumers in collection actions
- Federal laws that regulate credit-reporting agencies
- Federal laws that control credit-repair firms

With the failure of many banks during the Great Depression of the 1930s, the federal government jumped in with both feet to protect consumers from unethical and unsafe banking practices. Once the banks, savings and loans, finance companies, and mortgage companies were on relatively stable footing, the government continued to enact laws to ensure that consumers were treated fairly. Those efforts continue today with the latest legislation in 2004, the Fair and Accurate Credit Transactions Act (discussed later in this chapter).

Consumer-protection laws in the financial industry are regulated at the federal level because many of the companies do business across state lines and many of them are federally chartered institutions. States also have consumer laws, but here I look to the federal legislation to set the standards for most issues relating to credit and debt.

Title 15

Title 15 of the United States Code covers commerce and trade. Chapter 41 of Title 15 covers consumer credit protection.

Credit Cautions

Never let a creditor give you legal advice or interpret a law for you. Even if your account has been sent to a law firm for collection, it is likely you are not speaking with an attorney. Even if you are, that attorney works for your creditor, not you. He is not trying to help you; he is merely doing his job to collect this debt for his client.

Three main pieces of legislation in Title 15 are relevant to our discussions in this book: the Fair Credit Reporting Act, the Consumer Credit Protection Act, and the Truth in Lending Act. All these acts of legislation have had several amendments passed in subsequent years, some of which have become more famous than the original bill, such as the Fair Debt Collection Act, which amended the Consumer Credit Protection Act. Let's look at each of these laws in turn.

Fair Credit Reporting Act

The Fair Credit Reporting Act (15 U.S.C. §§ 1681–1681(v), as amended) regulates the information consumer-reporting agencies collect for distribution. It stipulates that the information may be distributed only to people or companies presenting a purpose specified in the act, such as credit granting, insurance, and employment. In addition, it states that the reporting agencies have a duty to investigate disputed information and to verify other information automatically. Purchasers of the information must notify consumers if an adverse action was taken, based on the information provided, and must state which reporting agency provided the information. The act allows free reports to be requested at certain events, such as denial of credit, employment, or insurance, based on information provided in a report.

The entire text of the law that governs the behavior of credit-reporting agencies can be found online at www.ftc.gov/os/statutes/fcra.htm.

To Your Credit _____

When you see the strange markings in parentheses after a law that look like 15 U.S.C. §§ 1681–1681(v), you can read them as "Title 15 of the United States Code, Sections 1681 to 1681(v)." Whenever you see a law summarized, don't be afraid to look up the law on the Internet and see what it really says.

Fair and Accurate Credit Transactions Act of 2003

The Fair and Accurate Credit Transactions Act, often called the FACT Act, took effect in September 2005. It expanded the role of the Fair Credit Reporting Act to protect consumers and also addressed the needs of consumers victimized by identity thieves.

The main change that most consumers enjoy is the provision that allows each consumer to receive a copy of his credit file from the three national reporting agencies on a yearly basis at no charge. A central phone number, e-mail address, and PO box were established and are maintained by a contracted company. This company, separate from the three credit-reporting agencies, takes a request for a report and forwards it on to one, two, or all three of the bureaus. You will receive the reports you request either online or through the mail if they cannot verify your identity online. You are entitled to one report every 365 days from each bureau, and you don't have to order them at the same time.

To Your Credit

It's not necessary to memorize these laws or even read them in their entirety. It is important to know they exist so you can refer to them when you feel you are being treated unfairly. Most attorneys don't spend any time learning or advising about these laws because, frankly, little money is made in this area. It's up to you to do your homework, consult with consumer-protection agencies, and then track down an attorney who does have some expertise if you believe a law has been broken and has caused you damage.

Consumer Credit Protection Act

The Consumer Credit Protection Act was sweeping legislation that is represented throughout Chapter 41 of Title 15. I summarize only the sections of the law that are most relevant to our discussion.

Equal Credit Opportunity Act

The Equal Credit Opportunity Act (15 U.S.C. §§ 1691–1691f, as amended) names specific characteristics of a potential borrower that a creditor cannot use to screen for granting credit. These characteristics are race, religion, national origin, gender, marital status, and age. It also lists two actions that cannot be held against a potential borrower: receipt of public assistance and the good-faith exercise of any rights under the Consumer Credit Protection Act. The creditor must provide the applicant with the underlying reason for denying him credit.

The entire text of this law is on the Legal Information Institute website: www4.law.cornell. edu/uscode/15/1691.html.

Fair Debt Collections Practices Act

The Fair Debt Collections Practices Act (15 U.S.C. §§ 1692–1692o, as amended) prohibits certain deceptive or abusive behavior of third-party collectors of consumer debts. Among the conduct prohibited is calling at odd hours, making repeated telephone calls, threatening legal action they don't plan to follow through on, and discussing the debt with others. These laws are often misquoted, and it is often believed they apply to the original creditor as well. Most collection departments have standardized their practices so they are in compliance with this law, even though it doesn't apply to them.

You can find the entire text of this law online at www.ftc.gov/bcp/edu/pubs/consumer/credit/cre27. pdf.

Credit Repair Organizations Act

The Credit Repair Organizations Act (15 U.S.C. §§ 1679–1679j) was created in response to the quickly growing credit-repair industry in the mid-1990s. It requires certain disclosures by credit-repair firms to potential customers. It bars the practice of requiring payment up front, and it requires written contracts and specific cancellation rights.

To view the entire text of the act online, go to www. ftc.gov/os/statutes/croa/croa.htm.

Truth in Lending Act

The Truth in Lending Act (15 U.S.C. §§ 1601–1667f, as amended) requires creditors to disclose all finance charges, including the charges expressed as an annual percentage rate (APR). The act also mandates a three-day right of rescission for certain loans, such as home equity loans, which take a security interest in the consumer's residence. It also regulates how creditors may advertise their loan provisions.

Go to www4.law.cornell.edu/uscode/15/1601.html to begin viewing the provisions of the Truth in Lending Act. Additional sections, through 1667, follow on the website.

Credit Cautions

Several laws mandate complete disclosure of credit information to consumers, but they do you no good if you don't read these disclosures and ask questions. You won't initially understand all of the mumbo-jumbo and fine print, so keep asking questions until you do.

Fair Credit Billing Act

The Fair Credit Billing Act (15 U.S.C. §§ 1666–1666j) amended the Truth in Lending Act to more closely govern the behavior of credit card company billing practices. This amendment gives consumers protections while they are disputing a billing error. It also requires that creditors post payments promptly and acknowledge consumer billing complaints in writing.

The Federal Trade Commission includes the entire text of the law on its website at www.ftc.gov/os/statutes/fcb/fcb.pdf.

Home Equity Loan Consumer Protection Act

This amendment to the Truth in Lending Act regulates home equity loans, requiring certain disclosures and imposing limitations. It is codified in scattered sections of the U.S. Code, particularly 15 U.S.C. §§ 1637 and 1647.

Home Ownership and Equity Protection Act

The Home Ownership and Equity Protection Act (15 U.S.C. § 1639) amendment to the Truth in Lending Act is one of many attempts to manage the rise in predatory lending practices. This act requires disclosure and prohibits equity stripping and other abusive practices on high-cost mortgages.

Consumer Leasing Act

Another amendment to the Truth in Lending Act designed to protect consumers, the Consumer Leasing Act (15 U.S.C. §§ 1667–1667f, as amended) requires that certain lease costs and terms be disclosed. It regulates the size of penalties that can be imposed for delinquency and default.

Using Laws to Your Advantage

Reading laws is about as exciting as watching paint dry, except when they create opportunities for you to take charge of a situation. The Federal Trade Commission, your attorney general's office, and other consumer-advocate groups can help you determine whether any laws have been broken. Attorneys who specialize in credit issues can also be of help if you think you've spotted a violation. If you believe you've been harmed by the illegal actions of one of your creditors, an attorney can advise you on steps you might be able to take.

The Least You Need to Know

- Creditors are mandated to disclose all relevant information to you regarding a credit transaction.
- Credit bureaus operate under strict regulations to ensure the accuracy of your credit file and repair inaccurate information when notified.

- Credit bureaus may give your credit report only to parties with a legitimate purpose, some of whom must get your written consent before requesting a report and all of whom must tell you if they used that information to make a decision adverse to your interests.

- Regulated by federal law, third-party collectors must treat you honestly and fairly.

Chapter 13

Form Letters and Telephone Scripts

In This Chapter

- How to negotiate repayment and credit-report references with creditors
- Sample letters to challenge errors and improve your credit standing
- Suggested phone scripts to deal with collectors
- Strategies to communicate with credit bureaus

The mere idea of navigating those seemingly endless automated phone trees at large corporations sends most of us into hibernation:

Press 1 if you already have your problem solved.

Press 2 if you have no hope of getting us to solve it.

Although these interactions often leave you feeling frustrated and empty-handed, you can take some steps to keep more control and get better outcomes. Use some of the suggestions for phone and written communication in this chapter, and see what works for you.

Communicating With Creditors

For years, large, faceless corporations have been playing the "Who'd you talk to?" game. You would call and talk to a seemingly helpful and informed person, who assured you your problem had been resolved. When you discovered two weeks later that the problem wasn't resolved and called back, you were met with the question "Who did you talk to?" Then you found out that the person doesn't exist, doesn't have the power to do what he promised, or just didn't do it. In any case, you can't talk to *that* person again!

To Your Credit

The process of managing your credit report can become complicated if you don't document whom you speak with and what you send them. Make a new file folder for each problem that you hope to resolve, and keep copies of everything.

Phone Calls

Communicating with creditors can be difficult. The chances of ever talking with the same person twice are less than those of winning the lotto. If you send a fax, an e-mail, or a letter, who will actually read it and respond is an even bigger mystery. Calling to follow up is usually futile.

If it is important to you that your problem be resolved, it is important that you find out up front whom you are talking with. As soon as you get a real person—as opposed to an automated voice—on the phone, ask for the following information:

- Full name
- Title or ID number
- Department
- Location/city
- Callback number
- Prompts for that department

If the representative won't give you that information, ask to speak to a supervisor who will. If this is already your second or third attempt to solve a problem, immediately ask to speak with a supervisor. Most credit-company employees are required to allow you to speak to a supervisor on your first request. Sometimes the supervisor must call you back, but it's worth the wait to speak to a person you can talk to again.

Have all your documentation in front of you before you begin the call. It's very frustrating to make some progress with a helpful service rep, only to have to call back and start again with someone new because you didn't have all your information.

When you call, know what you want to accomplish from the call. Do you want information or action? Do you want the person to bend a rule for you? Do you want the person to accept an offer from you? Chances are better you'll get what you want if you know what that is.

In Writing

Many of your rights under the various consumer-protection laws (see Chapter 12) require you to notify the companies in writing of your wishes. My best advice is to call first and get the name of a real person to whom you can direct your correspondence. Tell this person your needs, and ask for cooperation. But always follow up with the same message in writing, sent to that person's attention, beginning with this phrase:

> Per our conversation of today, please fulfill the following request:

The next piece of information you should include in the letter is the statement of the problem or the facts as you know them. Include all dates, amounts, and descriptions of transactions or billing items. Attach copies of the statements or reports you are referring to with the items highlighted. If the person receiving your letter doesn't have to look long and hard for the supporting documentation, your inquiry or request will take much less time to process.

Next, state your request or the action you intend to take. Be specific. If you are offering to pay an amount to clear a debt, state how and when you will pay it. If you are requesting an item be researched, state when you need the information. Don't let people fill in any blanks themselves because they will always do it in their favor.

What you say and how you say it depends, of course, on what you're asking for. The best approach is to keep your letter simple and direct. In the following sections, I provide wording for some of the most common issues about which consumers communicate with creditors. You can customize these sample letters to reflect your individual situation.

Begin each of these sample letters with the following identifying information:

- Date
- Your name
- Name on account (if different)
- Billing address
- City/state/ZIP
- Phone number to contact you
- Best time to call
- Name of creditor
- Account number
- Name of third-party collector (if any)

- Collection account number (if any)
- Internal routing information (name of person you've dealt with before or the department handling this matter)

Error on Bill

On my statement dated _____, the following error occurred: _____ _____. I understand that you must acknowledge receipt of this notice within 30 days unless you correct the error before that. You have two billing cycles to correct this error or explain why you believe the item to be correct.

Erroneous Late Payment on Credit Report

I have reviewed a copy of my credit report from [Equifax, Experian, TransUnion], dated _____. It lists my payments to you as delinquent. I believe this is a false statement and request that you report only timely payments to the credit-reporting agencies for this account. If you believe the report is correct, please send me the documentation that supports this claim.

Request to Lower Monthly Payments

Due to adverse circumstances involving _____, I cannot pay the minimum monthly amount required on my credit contract with you. I can pay $_____ per month for _____ months.

I expect to resume the full payments when I
_____.

Please accept the reduced payments until then.
Thank you for your help during this difficult time.
Please contact me to let me know this is acceptable.

Request to Rewrite Loan

Due to _____, I find myself unable
to pay the monthly amount required by this loan
agreement. I would like the terms of the loan to
be rewritten to reduce the monthly payments to
$_____. Please call me to discuss new loan
terms.

Request to Accept Payoff for Less Than the Balance

Please find enclosed payment of $_____.
Acceptance of this check acknowledges payment in
full on the balance of the account.

Complaint About Unethical Collection Practices

You have retained the _____ collec-
tion agency to collect the outstanding balance on
my debt to you. I have been unable to pay this debt
because _____.

This collection agency has engaged in the following actions that are in violation of the Fair Debt
Collection Practices Act: _____

_____

_____.

In exchange for your written guarantee to permanently cease all collection efforts regarding this debt and permanently remove all negative entries regarding this debt from my credit reports at the three major credit-reporting agencies, I will waive the legal remedies I have available.

Request to Review Verified Derogatory Information

On my credit report from _____ , dated _____, my account with you shows the following incorrect information: _____ _____. The credit bureau has refused to remove this information, stating that you have verified the information with them. Please find attached documentation that disputes your reporting of my account.

Please remove this derogatory information from all three major reports within 20 days and send me confirmation that you have done this. You are currently damaging my credit and will be responsible for damages after the 20 days have passed.

Communicating With Collectors

Collectors: what a fun-loving bunch of folks to chat with! Chances are, they are fairly nice people when they go home for the evening, but while at work, they are paid to throw you off balance and get you to take actions that might not be in your best interest. Doing your homework and knowing what you need to accomplish is the key to staying in control of the communication.

On the Phone

When a collector calls you, he is more prepared to have a conversation than you are. Many dialing systems give a collector only a fraction of a second to see who he has just connected with, but he knows he's going to be asking you for a payment. It's much better if you call him. That way, you are the one who is prepared. He will be caught off guard, or possibly thrilled, that he actually has you on the phone.

Have the following information ready before you call:

- Name on the account
- Account number
- Balance you owe
- Next payment amount you can make
- The date you can make it

Don't forget to collect the same information about whom you are talking with that we discussed in the previous section. Many times, collection agencies will be happy to let you speak to the same person again. Depending upon the size of the agency, your account might actually be assigned to a specific employee.

The collector will attempt to learn a lot about you by asking many questions. You don't have to answer any of them. The standard verbiage they use is, "This is an effort to collect a debt. Any information received might be used for that purpose." All you need to tell them is what you need them to know, which is what you can afford to pay and what help you need from them.

Once you show a willingness to bring your account current or pay it off, you'll find many collectors have a lot of flexibility in how they can help you. They can lower interest rates, re-age accounts, settle for less than the full amount owed, and take other helpful actions.

In Writing

The following are some examples of letters you might need to write. Be sure to include the same identifying information covered in the previous section. Always copy the original creditor on any correspondence to a collection agency.

Negotiated Payment in Exchange for Improved Credit Reference

Unlike in the past, I am now able to pay the balance on this debt. I will pay you $ _____ within 30 days or $ _____ per month for _____ months if you agree to one of the following terms:

_____ If I pay this debt in full within 30 days, you will remove all negative information associated with this debt from my credit references at the three major credit bureaus.

_____ If I pay the debt monthly beginning within 30 days, you will re-age my account, showing no late payments as long as I make the monthly payments.

Please initial one of the above items and sign below. I will forward the first or full payment within 30 days of receipt.

Judgment Proof Notice to Collector

This letter is to notify you that I am *judgment proof*. I am aware that you might be awarded a judgment if you seek one, but I can claim my assets as exempt, and you would collect nothing under current law. I am not able to make payments on my account because I am not able to work enough to meet my basic expenses.

Please cease all collection activity you are currently engaged in or contemplating. I will respond to reasonable requests for information in writing, and I will notify you as my situation changes and I am able to resume payments on this account.

def•i•ni•tion

> To be **judgment proof** is to have no assets that can be seized and no wages that can be garnished.

Notice of Intention to File for Bankruptcy Protection

This is my written notice that I intend to file a petition for bankruptcy protection with the Federal Bankruptcy Court in the coming months. As you know, per this notice, you are prohibited from continuing any and all collection activities toward me in any form.

Request to Revert Collections to Original Creditor

This is notice of my desire to work with the original creditor to resolve the balance due on my account. I will not be communicating with you directly on this matter beyond this letter. Please cease all calls and letters. Please notify the creditor that I will be in touch with them on this matter.

Disputing the Validity of a Bill at a Collection Agency

This letter is notice of my dispute of the above-referenced bill you are attempting to collect. I believe your actions are in error because _____ _____. Please refer the debt back to the original creditor and notify them of my dispute. Please remove any reference to your collection action from my credit reports at the three major credit bureaus.

Notice to a Collection Agency to Cease Communications

Your collection agency has been contacting me by phone and through the mail to collect the above-referenced debt. Per my rights under 15 U.S.C. Section 1692C, this is my written notice to you to cease all future communication with me in writing or via telephone.

Communicating With Credit Bureaus

You must go through the third-party service to order your free annual report:

Annual Credit Report Request Services
PO Box 104281
Atlanta, GA 30374-5281
1-877-322-8228
www.annualcreditreport.com

Ordering your other reports has never been easier.
The Big Three all have websites where you can
order your reports and often have them delivered to
you electronically:

- www.experian.com
- www.equifax.com
- www.transunion.com

They also have toll-free numbers that allow you to
place your requests for copies of your reports.

- Experian: 1-888-397-3742
- Equifax: 1-800-685-1111
- TransUnion: 1-800-888-4213

In Writing

In some circumstances, you will want to write to
the credit bureaus and keep hard copies of your
requests. For example, if you are purchasing a
report and don't want to use a credit card to pay for
it, you'll need to send a check, along with a written
request, to the following:

- TransUnion, LLC
  Consumer Disclosure Center
  PO Box 1000
  Chester, PA 19022

- Experian
  PO Box 2002
  Allen, TX 75013

- Equifax
  PO Box 740241
  Atlanta, GA 30374

Whether you call, write, or order online, be prepared to give the following information:

- Full legal name
- Date of birth
- Social Security number
- Current address
- Previous addresses for five years

Requesting a Credit Report in Various Circumstances

Please provide me with a copy of my credit file for no fee because:

____ I was recently denied credit based on information provided by your credit-reporting agency on _____ by _____. I have attached the letter of denial.

____ I am unemployed and intend to apply for a job within the next 60 days.

____ I receive public assistance/welfare.

____ I believe there is erroneous information in my file due to fraud.

_____   I am requesting my annual free credit report.

Request to Investigate Items on a Report

Please investigate and correct the following items. I believe them to be inaccurate:

Personal information:

Error   *Corrected Information*

_____   _____

Accounts not belonging to me:

Creditor   *Account Number*

_____   _____

Payment history not accurate:

Creditor   *Account Number*

_____   _____

Items older than seven years:

Creditor's Name Account Number Date of Last Activity

_____ _____ _____

Inquiries older than two years:

Creditor   *Date of Inquiry*

_____   _____

Inquiries not authorized:

Creditor   *Date of Inquiry*

_____   _____

Accounts closed by me:

Creditor   *Account Number*

_____   _____

Please complete your investigation within 30 days of receipt of this letter, and remove the information if the creditor cannot verify it. Thank you for your prompt service.

Request to Remove Unverified Items

I have enclosed a copy of an original request to investigate several items on my credit report that I sent to you more than 30 days ago. You have not replied to this request, and I am now requesting that you remove those items and send me a corrected report. Also send a corrected report to anyone who has requested a report in the previous six months.

Request to Respond to Creditor Letter

Please find attached a letter from my creditor, _____. It states that information in my credit file is not accurate and should be corrected. Please respond appropriately to my request to correct this information. Please send me a copy of the corrected report and also send one to anyone who has requested a copy of my report in the last six months.

Request to Add Nonreporting Accounts to Report

The following accounts are missing from my credit file at your company. I have attached copies of my statements for your review. Please add these accounts to my report and send me an updated report.

Creditor: _____

Account Number: _____

Date Opened: _____

Credit Limit or Outstanding Balance: _____

Type of Account: _____

Request to Add Miscellaneous Information to Report

Please place the following information into my credit file. I have attached copies of verifying documentation.

Please send me an updated copy of my credit report. Please let me know if you are unable to complete this request.

Use the forms and scripts in this chapter to help you prepare communications strategies with each credit reference you need to talk with. Get the ball rolling soon because some issues might take time to resolve to your satisfaction.

The Least You Need to Know

- Gathering all your information and knowing what you want to accomplish before you write or call is the most important step toward making progress in reaching your credit goals.

- When speaking with a creditor or credit bureau on the phone, always get the name of the person you are speaking with, as well as that person's job title and direct contact information.

- You have several rights under federal law that you must invoke in writing. It is prudent to follow up all spoken communication with written verification.

- Always document any requests and keep good records to follow up with any communication.

Glossary

account classification System reporting agencies use to identify which type of account the consumer opened—for example, revolving account, installment loan, or mortgage.

account rating Term creditors use to refer to the relative status of your account. Each creditor might have its own internal rating system.

agent banks Smaller banks that serve as agents for larger banks in credit card services.

annual fee Flat amount to maintain a credit account, not based on the outstanding balance.

annual percentage rate (APR) Interest paid on a loan calculated on an annual basis. It might be higher than the interest rate because interest is compounded (charged on interest already incurred). According to the federal Truth in Lending Act, every consumer loan agreement must disclose the APR in large bold type.

asset Anything you own that has value and can be turned into cash.

authorized user   Anyone who is legally allowed to incur debt on a credit card in your name.

bad debt   An outstanding balance called due by the creditor but has not been paid.

balance transfer   The act of moving an outstanding balance from one credit card account to another.

bank card system   Credit card networks that allow smaller institutions to offer credit card products even though they cannot support all the services needed by themselves.

bankruptcy   Legal process in the federal court system that gives debtors protection from asset seizure when debts are in default. The court takes possession of the assets remaining and distributes them equitably among the creditors. The court trustees handle repayment of debts.

cash advance   Loan in cash received at a teller or ATM that becomes part of the outstanding balance on an already established credit account.

Chapter 7   Option under the bankruptcy code that allows debtors to have their assets liquidated to satisfy their debts completely.

Chapter 13   Option under the bankruptcy code that allows debtors to retain some assets and use their future earnings to repay their creditors, in part or in full.

charge off   Action taken by a creditor that declares a debt uncollectable and allows that creditor to expense the balance as a loss for business and tax purposes.

civil judgment   Decision by a court that a debt is owed and an order is issued to pay the debt to the creditor, enforceable by certain actions, such as garnishment of assets and wages in some states.

claim   Filing by a creditor in a bankruptcy case that states money owed by the debtor.

co-signer   Person who is contractually obligated to back a debt if the original signer is unable to.

collateral   Asset pledged to back a debt when the debt is incurred. It can be seized if the debtor defaults.

collection   Term commonly used by creditors to mean in default and actively pursued for payment.

collection agency   Company that contracts with creditors to pursue collection activities when a debt is not paid on time. A collection agency can also purchase the debt from the original creditor for a discount and collect the money for itself.

consolidation loan   Loan that combines and refinances other loans or debt. It is normally an installment loan designed to reduce the dollar amount of an individual's monthly payments.

consumer file   Record of all the credit histories collected by a credit-reporting agency.

consumer report Report summarizing the information held in the consumer file at a credit-reporting agency.

consumer statement Written statement placed on a credit report disputing or explaining circumstances surrounding a credit reference on the report.

credit agency/bureau Company that collects and sells information on consumer or business credit behavior. Four companies dominate the industry in the United States. For consumer reports: Experian, Equifax, and TransUnion. For business reports: Dun and Bradstreet.

credit analysis Process a creditor uses to decide which consumers to grant credit to.

credit bureau members/subscribers Businesses that pay a fee to belong to or do business with the credit bureaus and, therefore, are able to order the reports they produce.

credit capacity Amount of credit that a creditor determines a consumer can handle, given income and other obligations.

credit grantor/creditor Individual or business that extends a consumer/debtor a loan or line of credit.

credit history Summary of the manner in which a consumer handled credit contracts, reflecting how much he borrowed, whether he made payments on time, and how much he still owes.

credit limit   *See* credit line/line of credit.

credit line/line of credit   Amount of total debt that you can incur on a revolving credit account. Also referred to as your credit limit.

credit reference   Individual or business that has loaned a consumer money and is reporting to a credit bureau the experience on that account.

credit report   Report credit bureaus compile and sell, which can include (1) address history, (2) employment history, (3) public record information, (4) credit account histories, (5) credit report requests, and (6) consumer statements.

credit score   Number derived from a formula that calculates the probability that a person will honor a credit contract by making the payments on time per the contract. The most widely used was developed by Fair Isaac and is called the FICO score.

creditor   Granter of debt. Sometimes this company is not the company servicing or collecting the payments on the debt.

debtor   Individual or company that applies for and accepts a loan or a line of credit from a creditor.

default   When a customer doesn't make a required payment to a credit card account or otherwise violates the terms of the agreement between the credit card company and the customer.

delinquent   When an account is not paid per the contractual agreement, it is reported as delinquent on a credit report.

ding Indicator on a credit report that some or all companies looking at the report might find negative.

discharge Act of releasing the debtor of the obligation of a debt by the bankruptcy court.

Equal Credit Opportunity Act (ECOA) Federal law that protects consumers from credit discrimination on the basis of race, color, national origin, sex, marital status, age, or religion.

Equifax National credit-reporting agency that has affiliates in many areas. Also owns the Medical Information Bureau and other investigative companies.

Experian National credit-reporting agency; formerly owned by TRW, Inc.

Fair and Accurate Credit Transactions Act (FACT) Federal law that expanded the power of the Fair Credit Reporting Act to increase consumer rights.

Fair Credit Reporting Act (FCRA) Federal law that regulates the credit-reporting industry and attempts to control abuses of the process.

Fair Debt Collection Practices Act (FDCPA) Federal law passed in 1977 that outlawed unfair collection practices by third-party collectors, including debtor harassment.

Federal Trade Commission (FTC) Federal agency that regulates a variety of consumer processes, including credit reporting, credit repair, and identity theft.

FICO score (Fair Isaacs)   Objective methodology credit grantors use to determine how much, if any, credit to grant to an applicant. Some factors in scoring are income, assets, length of employment, length of living in one place, and past record of using credit.

finance charges   Price paid to a lender when borrowing money, based on a percentage of the outstanding balance, which is regulated by many states on various credit contracts.

fixed interest rate   Interest rate that does not fluctuate with general market conditions. There are fixed-rate mortgage (also known as conventional mortgages) and consumer installment loans, as well as fixed-rate business loans.

fixed rate   Set annual percentage rate that does not change in response to interest rate changes and conditions. With credit card accounts, this doesn't mean the rate cannot change—only that it won't change automatically with some external index.

foreclosure   Legal process that leads to the repossession and sale of real property pledged as collateral on a mortgaged debt.

good standing   Condition of a credit account that is currently paid as agreed.

grace period   (1) Time period during which no interest is charged on credit card usage. (2) Time period after a payment is due before a late fee is charged.

interest   Fee, stated as a percentage of the outstanding balance, a creditor charges for use of its money.

introductory rate   Annual percentage rate used to entice consumers to open an account, applicable for only a limited period of time. Also called a teaser rate.

late payment fee   Fee charged when a payment has not been received by the specified due date.

liability   Total amount a consumer owes on a debt.

lien   Interest in a piece of property that guarantees a debt.

loan   Exchange of funds with a promise to repay under certain terms, including time period, interest rate, and frequency of payments.

major bank   Bank that provides services to the agent banks in a chain.

minimum payment   Smallest payment that a customer can make each statement period to keep the account in good standing.

MOP   Manner of payment. Might head the column on a credit report that lists the payment history.

neutral   Account that is not rated on a credit report due to newness or some other reason; it is neither positive nor negative on the report.

nonverification   Lapse of the 30 days that a credit bureau is given under law to verify a debt at the consumer's request.

payment history   Summary of the payments made on a specific loan obligation, usually stated as how many payments were made on time, 30 days late, 60 days late, or 90 days late.

penalty rate   Higher APR the credit card company charges after the customer has made late payments, exceeded the credit limit, or otherwise failed to abide by the card-member agreement.

primary user   Debtor signed on an account who is primarily responsible for repaying the debt.

reaffirmation   Exclusion of a debt from a bankruptcy process, promising to pay the debt in full after the bankruptcy.

reasonable time   Amount of time a credit bureau has to respond to a consumer dispute—usually up to eight weeks.

repossession   Seizure of assets used to secure a debt when the debt becomes delinquent.

rule of 78s   Method of computing rebates of interest on installment loans. Its basis is the sum of the year's digits for determining the interest earned by the finance company for each month of a year, assuming equal monthly payments. It gets its name from the fact that the sum of the digits 1 through 12 is 78. Thus, interest is equal to 12/78ths of the total annual interest in the first month, 11/78ths in the second month, and so on.

secured credit card   Credit card backed by a savings account equal to or greater than the credit limit on the card.

stay   Act by the bankruptcy judge to stop all creditor action toward the debtor.

subscriber   Customer of the credit bureaus who may request credit reports.

teaser rate   *See* introductory rate.

TransUnion   National credit-reporting agency.

variable rate   Annual percentage rate that periodically goes up or down, based on fluctuations in market interest rates as reflected in a published index (such as the prime rate published in *The Wall Street Journal*).

write-off   Action taken by a creditor to consider a debt uncollectable, thereby taking a loss for tax purposes.

zero liability   When your credit card issuer assumes all liability for unauthorized purchases on your card. There may be restrictions on this feature, but it can be helpful if your account numbers are stolen.

Resources

I have gathered a variety of resources for you to take your quest for a healthy credit report in any direction you desire. Many of the websites listed here have additional links and resources for you to access. I have specifically excluded sites that didn't disclose, even upon request, their street address or phone number. Before you rely on the advice or information from any of them, understand who they are and why they exist.

Problem-Resolution Resources

Council of Better Business Bureaus
4200 Wilson Blvd., Suite 800
Arlington, VA 22203
www.bbb.org
703-276-0100

This membership organization promotes ethical business practices and provides referrals to the local office that serves the area where the company you are doing business with is located. It has brochures on a variety of consumer topics and can help to resolve issues evolving from identity theft.

National Association of Attorneys General (NAAG)

750 First St. NE, Suite 1100
Washington, DC 20002
www.naag.org
202-326-6000

A professional association of elected state attorneys general, this site provides links to each state's website, where you can find consumer-protection information specific to your state.

Federal Trade Commission (FTC)

CRC 240
Washington, DC 20580
www.ftc.gov
1-877-382-4357

This government agency supervises the activities of credit bureaus, repair clinics, and collection agencies. A wide variety of free booklets is also available.

FTC's Identity Theft Hotline

www.consumer.gov/idtheft
1-877-IDTHEFT (1-877-438-4338)

This hotline is charged with collecting complaints about identity theft at its regional offices. Counselors will take your complaint and advise you on steps to take. They also can provide an Identity Theft Affidavit that you can submit to your creditors.

Information and Education Resources

Consumer Information Center
Pueblo, CO 81009
www.pueblo.gsa.gov
1-800-FED-INFO (1-800-333-4636)

This federal government central distribution center provides consumer information. A catalog is available.

Credit.About
About, Inc.
249 W. 17th St.
New York, NY 10011
www.credit.about.com
212-849-2000

This interactive, educational, and informational site is designed to help consumers learn about credit and debt.

Consumer Action
717 Market St., Suite 310
San Francisco, CA 94103-2109
www.consumer-action.org
415-777-9635

A nonprofit consumer-advisory organization, it offers lists of secured cards and low-rate cards as well as dozens of other helpful online informational articles on every aspect of personal financial management.

Consumer Federation of America
1424 16th St. NW, Suite 604
Washington, DC 20036
www.consumerfederation.org
202-387-6121

This consumer-advocacy organization publishes booklets on a range of financial topics, available online or through the mail.

Credit.com
550 15th St., Suite 36b
San Francisco, CA 94103
www.credit.com
1-877-273-4273

The company provides education, information, and credit products and services, including credit reports and fraud alerts.

Credit Info Center
Web Nation, Inc.
7904 E. Chaparral Rd., Suite 110-604
Scottsdale, AZ 85250
www.creditinfocenter.com
1-877-933-6932

The site takes on the Big Three credit-reporting agencies, credit-counseling firms, and other anti-consumer organizations, providing opinions and links to resources. It also provides credit report consulting.

U.S. Public Interest Research Group
218 D St. NE
Washington, DC 20003
www.pirg.org
202-546-9707

This nonprofit political action group provides fact sheets on credit reports, bureaus, and identity theft.

Privacy Rights Clearinghouse
3100 5th Ave., Suite B
San Diego, CA 92103
www.privacyrights.org
619-298-3396

The organization provides fact sheets on a range of privacy topics and also provides support services for identity theft victims.

National Fraud Information Center
National Consumers League
1701 K St. NW, Suite 1200
Washington, DC 20006
www.fraud.org
1-800-876-7060

This hotline refers fraud complaints to the appropriate enforcement agency and also has information on how to protect yourself from fraud.

Identity Theft Resource Center
PO Box 26883
San Diego, CA 92196
www.idtheftcenter.org
858-693-7935

This nationwide nonprofit organization helps victims and informs consumers of prevention strategies.

Counseling Resources

Financial Recovery Institute
PO Box 178
San Anselmo, CA 94979
www.financialrecovery.com
1-877-224-9933

The organization provides referrals to financial-recovery counselors who can help consumers rework their relationship with money by taking both financial and emotional issues into account.

Institute of Consumer Financial Education (ICFE)
PO Box 34070
San Diego, CA 92163
www.icfe.info
619-239-1401

This comprehensive website offers individual counseling, educational programs, and brochures on a variety of credit and money-management topics. It also offers a credit repair and correction helpline.

Debtors Anonymous
General Service Office
PO Box 920888
Needham, MA 02492-0009
www.debtorsanonymous.org
781-453-2743

The association provides referrals to local support groups. It operates similarly to Alcoholics Anonymous, with members coaching and supporting other members through a 12-step program designed to change their attitudes and behaviors surrounding debt.

Association of Independent Consumer Credit Counseling Agencies (AICCCA)
PMB 626
11350 Random Hills Rd., Suite 800
Fairfax, VA 22030
www.aiccca.org
703-934-6118

This trade association lists consumer credit counseling agencies not usually affiliated with the National Foundation for Consumer Credit.

National Foundation for Consumer Credit (NFCC)
8611 2nd Ave., Suite 100
Silver Spring, MD 20910
www.nfcc.org
1-800-388-2227

A trade association for consumer credit counseling agencies, it can refer you to an office in your area.

Financial Services

American Express Consumer Affairs Office
American Express Company
801 Pennsylvania Ave. NW, Suite 650
Washington, DC 20004
www.americanexpress.com
1-800-528-4800

Consumer website/office that discusses all personal credit issues related to cards issued by American Express.

Discover Cardmember Services
Discover Card
PO Box 30943
Salt Lake City, UT 84130-0943
www.discovercard.com
1-800-347-2683

This consumer website/office discusses all personal credit issues related to cards issued by Discover.

Your Credit Card Companies.Com
1220 L St. NW, Suite 100-375
Washington, DC 20005-4018
www.yourcreditcardcompanies.com
1-800-337-0590

This trade association of financial-service companies has banded together to increase consumer understanding of how the industry works. The site is a centralized resource for consumers and teachers of credit education.

MasterCard International Public Relations
MasterCard
200 Purchase St.
Purchase, NY 10577
www.mastercard.com
1-800-MC-ASSIST (1-800-622-7747)

This company is behind the MasterCard credit card your bank issues to you. For most concerns you would speak with the financial institution directly, but if you can't find an institution or it's not responding, MasterCard might be able to assist you.

www.creditalk.com

This is a very nice website designed by MasterCard for kids and young adults who are just learning how to manage money.

Visa Consumer Relations
PO Box 194607
San Francisco, CA 94119-4607
www.usa.visa.com
1-800-VISA-911 (1-800-847-2911)

This company is behind the Visa credit card your bank issues to you. The site offers direct Visa promotions, but for other questions and problems, contact your lending institution.

www.practicalmoneyskills.com

A site developed by Visa with educational partners teaches consumers, students, teachers, and parents the basics of financial literacy.

CardTrak
PO Box 1700
Frederick, MD 21702
www.cardweb.com
1-800-344-7714

The company sells lists of low-rate cards, rebate cards, gold cards, and secured cards. There is a small fee for purchasing each list.

Banxquote
BanxCorp
6 Palmer Ave.
Scarsdale, NY 10583
www.banxquote.com
914-722-1600

This site gives real-time interest rate comparisons on all types of credit and savings products.

Bankrate, Inc.
11811 U.S. Hwy. 1
North Palm Beach, FL 33408
www.bankrate.com/brm/ccstep.asp
561-630-2400

This industry watchdog provides credit card information to help consumers make wise choices and understand their rights.

E-Loan
6230 Stoneridge Mall Dr.
Pleasanton, CA 94588
www.eloan.com
1-888-533-5333

This online loan source provides its own credit scoring, with advice on how to improve your credit score.

Credit-Reporting Agencies

Intersections
PO Box 222455
Chantilly, VA 20153-2455
www.intersections.com
1-800-695-7536

The agency provides, for one fee, a combined credit report from all three bureaus, reformatted to be easier to read.

ChexSystems
Attn: Consumer Relations
7805 Hudson Rd., Suite 100
Woodbury, MN 55125
www.chexhelp.com
1-800-428-9623

This credit-reporting agency reports only on consumer behavior relating to checking account and ATM problems.

True Credit
TrueLink (TransUnion)
100 Cross St., Suite 202
San Luis Obispo, CA 93401
www.truecredit.com
1-800-493-2392

Consumer-oriented services help you obtain your reports, correct errors, and prevent identity theft.

Fair Isaac Consumer Credit Information
Fair Isaac Corporation
200 Smith Ranch Rd.
San Rafael, CA 94903
www.fairisaac.com
www.myfico.com
415-472-2211

This company designed and sells the scoring tool used by many creditors. The site explains this system.

Equifax Personal Solutions
Equifax Information Services, LLC
PO Box 740256
Atlanta, GA 30374
www.guardmycredit.com
1-800-685-1111

This company provides you with your reports and notifications of any activity on your reports and can also help you get off junk-mail and telemarketing lists. Additional services include identity theft insurance and reports that help you lower your car and homeowner insurance rates.

Experian Consumer Services
CreditExpert
PO Box 1909
Orange, CA 92865
www.creditexpert.com
1-866-673-0140

This consumer site, offered by Experian, sells credit-monitoring and other services.

Laws Governing Credit and Credit Reporting

Fair Debt Collection Practices Act
www.ftc.gov/os/statutes/fdcpa/fdcpact.htm

At the Federal Trade Commission website, the entire text of the law that governs the behavior of third-party collectors.

Fair Credit Billing Act
www.ftc.gov/os/statutes/fcb/fcb.pdf

At the Federal Trade Commission website, the entire text of the law that amended the Truth in Lending Act to more closely govern the behavior of credit card company billing practices.

Credit Repair Organizations Act
www.ftc.gov/os/statutes/croa/croa.htm

At the Federal Trade Commission website, the entire text of the law that amended the Consumer Credit Protection Act to more closely govern the behavior of credit-repair organizations.

Equal Credit Opportunities Act
www4.law.cornell.edu/uscode/15/1691.html

At the Legal Information Institute website, the entire text of the section of federal law that prevents discrimination on the basis of race, gender, marital status, and other prohibited demographic information.

Fair Credit Reporting Act
www.ftc.gov/os/statutes/fcra.htm

At the Federal Trade Commission website, the entire text of the law that governs the behavior of credit-reporting agencies.

Truth in Lending Act
www.ftc.gov/os/statutes/fcra.htm

At the Legal Information Institute website, the entire text of the law that governs how information must be disclosed to consumers when entering into debt contracts.

Index